Low & Slow Cooking

PAGE STREET
PUBLISHING CO.

Low & Slow Cooking

60 Hands-Off Recipes That Are Worth the Wait

Robyn Almodovar
winner of Chopped *and* Cutthroat Kitchen

PAGE STREET
PUBLISHING CO.

Table of *Contents*

Introduction   7

Family Favorites   9
Not Your Ordinary Pot Roast   11
Sunday Gravy   12
Puerto Rican Chicken Stew   15
Not Yo Momma's Meatloaf   18
Grandma's Beef Stew   21
Momma Duke's Chicken Tacos   22
Ropa Vieja   25
Take That Chicken and Throw It on Top of a Beer   26

The Best Dinner Ideas   29
Standout Pork Shank with
Broccoli and Brussels Sprout Slaw   31
Cassoulet, My Way   33
Rich and Velvety Coq au Vin   37
The Best Indoor Brisket   38
Citrus-Smoked Salmon   41
Chicken Chasseur   42

Nothing Baby about These Ribs with
Burrata and Peach Salad   45
Smoked Ham Shank with Watermelon Relish   47
Pork Belly This   51
Slow-Roasted Cod with Chimichurri   52
Slow-Roasted Pork Butt with Sweet & Spicy Glaze   55
Slow-Smoked Beef Ribs   56
Soy-Marinated Short Ribs with Asian Slaw   59
Sausage & Gravy Pizza   61
Set-and-Forget It Quiche   65
Lamb Shank with Orange Gremolata   66
Duck Confit with Apple & Celeriac Salad   68
Pork Belly Tacos   71

My Favorite Things to Eat in a Bowl   73
Beefed Up Bourguignon   75
Piggy Mac   76
Lamb & Squash Soup   79
Smoked Corn Chowder   80
Healthy, Hearty Spinach, Sausage & Bean Soup   83
All about That Bisque   84

Party Favorites 87

Game Day Wings 89
The Best Meat Sliders Around 90
Short Rib Chili with Cornbread 93
Sticky Drumsticks with Watermelon Salad 95
2-Steppin' Spare Ribs 99
Slow-Roasted Pork Sandwich 100
Ropa Vieja Empanadas 103

Great Slow Side Dishes 105

Dutch Oven Bread 107
Puerto Rican Red Beans 108
Kickin' Cornbread 111
Cuban Black Beans 112
Sweet and Spicy Baked Beans 115
Southern Collard Greens 116
Smoked & Grilled Corn Relish 119
My Momma's Mushrooms 120

It's All about the Basics 123

My Famous Wing Sauce 125
Classic Crema 126
Cilantro-Lime Crema 129
Smoked Salsa Verde 130
Smoky Salsa 133
Slow and Low Beef Stock 134
Deep-Flavor Chicken Stock 136
Go-To Vegetable Broth 137
The Best BBQ Sauce 139

Desserts, Please! 141

Chocolate Pot de Crème 143
Rocky Road Cake 144
Gooey Monkey Bread 147
Deep-Fried Bread Pudding 150
Slow-Cooked Blueberry Cobbler 153

Acknowledgments *154*
About the Author *155*
Index *156*

Introduction

I have always loved cooking because it's a way to be closer to my people. In my adolescent years, my sister and I had to cook every night in order to help our mother. When I visited my grandmother during the summer, I used to roll meatballs right alongside her for Sunday gravy. Even now, I spend most of my time in the kitchen making meals with friends and family.

Cooking may have started off as a chore but it quickly transformed into a hobby, and then later my biggest passion. I went to culinary school to hone my craft and then started my own food truck, Palate Party. I even competed on *Hell's Kitchen*, *Chopped* and *Cutthroat Kitchen*!

Over the years, I have always asked myself: What is it about food that leaves people wanting more? This simple question has haunted me for some time now. But over the years, I discovered the reason—food transports you to special moments in your life. One single morsel, or even a scent, has the ability to bring me back: right back to my summers with my grandma, weeknights with my sister or my early years in culinary school, even. To me, food ignites an emotional response within myself. Food can heal, excite, inspire and unite even the worst of enemies, which led me to create this cookbook.

The most memorable meals are the ones that are made with love. These recipes may take more time, but that's the point. The longer you work on them, the better the flavor is. And when you serve it to your special someone, they'll be able to tell how much time and effort you put into the dish. And maybe years from now, when they get a whiff of one of the ingredients, they'll be transported back to that time you made them that standout meal.

Roby Almodovar

Family
Favorites

··

In this chapter, you will find some of my family's favorite recipes. These dishes bring back memories of my family and me bonding over great food and conversation. I remember sitting around the kitchen table, watching my mom cook. Now, I am doing the cooking and now my mother can finally relax. One particular standout is my Sunday Gravy (page 12). You don't want to miss the layers of flavor in this recipe.

Not Your Ordinary Pot Roast

My sister and I loved pot roast while growing up—just not my mother's. My sister's best friend's mom was like an extension of our family and her pot roast was bangin'. I mastered the recipe in my early twenties and still cook it to this day. This right here is the tenderest pot roast you will ever stick your fork into. You will want to have leftovers because day two is the best day to eat this, when all the flavors have set and married together.

Serves 6 to 8

This can be cooked 2 ways: in the oven or on your stovetop. You decide.

For the oven method, preheat your oven to 225°F (110°C). Meanwhile, heat a Dutch oven on the stovetop over medium to high heat. Heavily season your chuck roast on all sides with the salt and pepper. Add the olive oil to the pot and sear the roast on both sides for around 5 minutes per side, or until golden brown. Remove the roast from the pot and set aside.

Add your onions, carrots and celery to the pot and cook until they are caramelized, about 7 to 8 minutes. Deglaze the pot with the red wine, making sure you scrape the bottom to get up all the yumminess. Return the chuck roast to the pot. Add the potatoes, rosemary, thyme and beef stock. Bring to a boil. Cover and transfer to the oven. Roast for 5 hours, or until fork-tender.

For the stovetop method, start everything as you would for the oven method and instead of putting it in the oven, put it on the back burner on low heat for 4 to 5 hours. Check at 4 hours to make sure it is tender. If not, return it to the heat for another hour.

Goes great on a hoagie—that's right, you read correctly.

1 (2- to 3-lb [905-g to 1.4-kg]) chuck roast

2 tbsp (36 g) salt

2 tbsp (12 g) freshly ground black pepper

2 tbsp (30 ml) olive oil

2 yellow onions, halved

6 carrots, peeled and cut in half

4 ribs celery, cut in half

6 tbsp (90 ml) red wine

2 Idaho potatoes, peeled and large diced

3 sprigs rosemary

3 sprigs thyme

4 cups (946 ml) beef stock (homemade [page 134] or store-bought)

Sunday Gravy

While I was growing up, my nanny used to make this for us every Sunday. It was started early in the morning and finished in midafternoon. The part I enjoyed as a kid was rolling the meatballs and throwing them in the gravy. That was my job and I looked forward to rolling the balls on Sundays. It was one of the most special bonding experiences with my nanny. This recipe is slow and low, but I promise it's worth the wait!

Serves 8

Prepare the gravy: Heat a Dutch oven over medium heat, then add the olive oil. Once it is heated, add the mild and spicy Italian sausages. Sear the sausages for 1 minute, or until all sides are evenly cooked with a light brown color, then remove from the pot and set aside. Next, season the beef neck bones with the salt and black pepper, place them in the pot and sear on all sides until golden brown, 3 minutes per side. Once cooked, remove from the pot and set aside with the sausages.

Add the crushed garlic and the onion to the pot and sauté until the onion is slightly translucent, about 3 minutes.

Add the red pepper flakes and stir around for 1 minute to open up the flakes. Add the crushed tomatoes to the pot. As for the whole tomatoes, crush them in your hands and then add them to the pot.

Return the cooked sausages and neck bones to the pot, then add the dried basil, granulated garlic, Parmesan cheese and balsamic vinegar. Stir for 45 seconds, or until mixed, and let the mixture come to a simmer.

(Continued)

Gravy

1 tbsp (15 ml) olive oil

2 mild Italian sausages

2 spicy Italian sausages

3 beef neck bones

1 tbsp (18 g) salt, or to taste

1 tsp freshly ground black pepper

3 cloves garlic, crushed

¼ large white onion, diced

1 tsp red pepper flakes

2 (16-oz [455-g]) cans crushed tomatoes

1 (16-oz [455-g]) can whole peeled tomatoes

1½ tsp (1 g) dried basil

1 tbsp (9 g) granulated garlic

¼ cup (25 g) grated Parmesan cheese

2 tsp (10 ml) balsamic vinegar

Sunday Gravy
continued

As you're waiting for your gravy to simmer, start your meatballs: In a large bowl, combine the ground chuck, beaten eggs, Parmesan cheese, red pepper flakes, dried basil, granulated garlic, balsamic vinegar, bread crumbs, fresh basil, salt and cold water. Gently mix until everything is incorporated. Cover with plastic wrap and place in the fridge until the gravy begins to simmer, 5 to 7 minutes.

Once the gravy is simmering, roll the chilled meatball mixture into twenty to twenty-five 1½-inch (4-cm) balls. As you roll the meatballs, slowly drop them into the gravy (Yes, you read correctly. No searing!), starting from the top of the Dutch oven (12 o'clock) and being sure to give your gravy a stir before you add the meatballs, to prevent breakage. In this manner, continue to add the meatballs as you form them, working your way around the pot, making sure they are not on top of one another. Once all the meatballs have been added, lower the heat to low. Cover tightly and let the gravy cook for about 4 hours, stirring once every hour. Before serving, tear up the basil leaves and stir into the sauce.

Goes great over pasta!

Note: To chiffonade herbs, place the leaves on top of one another and roll them up. Then, slice widthwise across the roll to cut it into small strips.

Meatballs

1½ lb (680 g) ground chuck

2 large eggs, beaten

½ cup (50 g) grated Parmesan cheese

1 tbsp (4 g) red pepper flakes

1 tbsp (2 g) dried basil

1 tbsp (9 g) granulated garlic

1 tsp balsamic vinegar

1 cup (115 g) bread crumbs

3 leaves fresh basil, chiffonaded (see Note)

1½ tsp (9 g) salt

1 cup (240 ml) cold water

4 basil leaves

Puerto Rican Chicken Stew

This brings me back to my childhood summer days in Orlando with my grandparents. This was one of my grandmother's favorite dishes to make for us while we were growing up. She said it made us strong. From the sweetness of the onions to the tanginess of the olives and cooking wine, this traditional Puerto Rican dish will bring you right back to the island. Letting the stew cook for this long means the chicken will become so tender and rich with flavors that it will have you going back for seconds. I took my grandmother's version and added a few touches of my own.

Serves 6

In a food processor, combine the bell peppers, garlic, onion, cilantro and culantro and pulse for 1 minute. Add the vinegar, olive brine and tomato paste, pulse once, then set aside.

In a small bowl, combine the annatto, salt, black pepper, granulated garlic, onion powder and cumin. Use this mixture to season your chicken evenly on all sides.

(Continued)

¼ red bell pepper, seeded and chopped

¼ green bell pepper, seeded and chopped

2 cloves garlic, smashed

½ white onion, chopped

¼ bunch cilantro

2 culantro leaves

1 tsp red wine vinegar

2 tbsp (30 ml) olive brine

1 tbsp (16 g) tomato paste

1 tsp annatto powder

1 tbsp (18 g) salt

1 tsp freshly ground black pepper

2 tsp (6 g) granulated garlic

2 tsp (5 g) onion powder

1 tsp ground cumin

Puerto Rican Chicken Stew
continued

Heat a large sauté pan over medium-high heat. Add the oil, then sear the chicken on all sides until golden brown, about 2 minutes per side.

Add the reserved pepper mixture to the chicken and cook for 5 minutes, stirring frequently. Deglaze the pan with the cooking wine and bring to a simmer. Add the chicken stock and bring to a boil. Remove from the heat and transfer the mixture to a 6- to 8-quart (5.7- to 7.6-L) slow cooker.

Add your potatoes, olives, bay leaves and oregano. Set the heat to LOW and cook for 7 hours. Remove the bay leaves and serve with rice and pita.

1½ lb (680 g) bone-in chicken wings, breasts, thighs or legs (If using breast or thighs, cut breast into medium-sized chunks and the thighs in half)

Olive oil, for sautéing

2 tbsp (30 ml) red cooking wine

2 qt (1.9 L) chicken stock (homemade [page 136] or store-bought)

4 yellow potatoes, peeled, cut into quarters and soaked in water

10 pimiento-stuffed olives

2 bay leaves

¼ tsp dried oregano

Not Yo Momma's Meatloaf

I hated meatloaf when I was younger. My mother would always tell me it's like a meatball or a hamburger—wrong. I realized the reason I didn't like it was that it was dry. With the slow and low technique, I guarantee this will be the juiciest meatloaf you've ever had.

Serves 4

Preheat your oven to 175°F (80°C). Butter a baking sheet or spray with butter spray.

In a sauté pan, heat the oil over medium heat and sweat the onion and celery until they are lightly caramelized, 4 to 5 minutes. Transfer them to a blender and puree.

In a large bowl, combine the eggs, bread crumbs, Worcestershire sauce, salt, minced garlic, granulated garlic, ¼ cup (60 ml) of the ketchup and the pureed mixture and mix well.

Crumble in the ground beef, using your fingers. Gently mix everything together. Do not overmix. Either put into a loaf pan (spray it first) or make a loaf with your hands and place on the prepared baking sheet. Brush the remaining ¼ cup (60 ml) of ketchup on top of the meatloaf. Place in the oven and cook for 6 hours. When the ketchup on top looks like a crust, it is done.

When you remove the meatloaf from the oven, make sure you let it cool down for at least 15 minutes before cutting.

Goes great with whipped mashed potatoes and green beans.

Butter or butter spray, for baking sheet

1 tbsp (15 ml) oil

½ cup (80 g) small-diced onion

½ cup (60 g) small-diced celery

2 large eggs

1 cup (115 g) Italian-seasoned bread crumbs

½ tsp Worcestershire sauce

2 tbsp (36 g) salt

2 tbsp (20 g) minced garlic

1 tbsp (9 g) granulated garlic

½ cup (120 ml) ketchup, divided

1½ lb (680 g) ground beef (80/20 blend)

Grandma's Beef Stew

While growing up, I would go to Florida every summer to visit my grandparents. The one dish that I was always looking forward to was my grandma's beef stew. She had a garden in the back of her house and that was where all of her culantro came from. The culantro in this dish brings another level of flavor that you will love.

Serves 6

Preheat your oven to 225°F (110°C). On the stovetop, heat a Dutch oven over medium heat.

Meanwhile, in a food processor, combine half of the onion with the culantro, cilantro, 2 of the garlic cloves and the bell pepper. Pulse until smooth. Transfer the pepper mixture to a large bowl. Add 1 tablespoon (15 ml) of the olive oil and stir. Add the cubed chuck meat to the bowl and mix well.

When the Dutch oven is hot, add the remaining 2 tablespoons (30 ml) of olive oil to the pot, then add your meat and sear on all sides until golden brown, 7 to 9 minutes total.

Remove the meat and set aside on a plate. Add the remaining half of the onion and sauté until translucent, about 3 minutes. Add the carrot and remaining garlic clove and cook for 2 minutes. Deglaze the pot with the red wine and scrape up the bits on the bottom. Return the meat to the pot. Add the cumin, granulated garlic, onion powder, turmeric, salt, pepper and annatto and stir to make sure everything is incorporated. Add your beef stock, bay leaves, potatoes, stuffed olives, tomato sauce and white vinegar. Cover, place in the oven and cook for 6 hours, or until the meat is tender. Remove the bay leaves before serving.

Goes great with tostones, which you can find at your local grocery store in the freezer section.

1 yellow onion, sliced, divided

2 leaves culantro

½ bunch cilantro

3 cloves garlic, smashed, divided

1 red bell pepper, seeded and large diced

3 tbsp (45 ml) olive oil, divided

2 lb (905 g) chuck roast, cut into 1" (2.5-cm) cubes

1 carrot, sliced into rounds

¼ cup (60 ml) red wine

1 tsp ground cumin

2 tsp (6 g) granulated garlic

2 tsp (5 g) onion powder

½ tsp ground turmeric

1½ tbsp (28 g) kosher salt

1 tsp freshly ground black pepper

1 tsp annatto powder

2 cups (475 ml) beef stock (homemade [page 134] or store-bought)

2 bay leaves

2 Idaho potatoes, medium diced

½ cup (50 g) pimiento-stuffed olives

1 (8-oz [227-g]) can tomato sauce

1 tbsp (15 ml) white vinegar

Momma Duke's Chicken Tacos

When my mom makes this, we usually eat five or six tacos each. No joke. I remember my nephew eating a record of nine. Needless to say, this is a family recipe and a family favorite. This recipe comes from my dad's side. The tacos are a bit bold with the taste of the culantro really coming through. The flavors have depth with hints of heat at the end. This is one dish that my mom *must* make when I go home for a visit. I am sure it will become one of your family favorites as well.

Serves 6

In a large stockpot, heat 1 tablespoon (15 ml) of the olive oil over medium to high heat. Add the onion and sauté until translucent, about 3 minutes. Add the chicken pieces and cover with the chicken stock. Bring to a boil, then lower the heat to a simmer. When the chicken is cooked, about 1 hour, remove it from the pot and let it cool down on a plate.

Add the tomato paste, chili powder, onion powder, garlic powder, cayenne, cumin, oregano, salt and black pepper to the pot.

In a blender, blend the chipotles with their sauce into a fine puree. Add 2 tablespoons (30 ml) of the puree to the pot and reserve the rest for another use.

In a food processor, combine the bell pepper, cilantro, hot sauce, remaining tablespoon (15 ml) of olive oil and the culantro. Process to a puree and add to the pot. Lower the heat to low and let cook, covered, for 1 hour 30 minutes. While this is cooking, lightly shred the cooled chicken meat. At the 1½-hour point, add the chicken to the pot and cook, covered, for 45 minutes.

Remove the pot from the heat.

In a sauté pan, heat your tortillas lightly on both sides over low heat. Remove from the pan. Time to eat. Garnish your tacos with cilantro, radishes and lime wedges.

2 tbsp (30 ml) olive oil, divided

1 onion, diced

1 (3- to 5-lb [1.4- to 2.3-kg]) chicken, cut into 8 pieces

4 cups (946 ml) chicken stock (homemade [page 136] or store-bought)

2 tbsp (32 g) tomato paste

1 tsp chili powder

1 tsp onion powder

1 tsp garlic powder

1 tsp cayenne pepper

1 tsp ground cumin

1 tsp dried oregano

1 tbsp (18 g) salt

1 tsp freshly ground black pepper

1 (7-oz [198-g]) can chipotle peppers in adobo sauce

1 green bell pepper, seeded and diced

½ bunch cilantro, plus more for garnish

3 dashes of hot sauce

2 leaves culantro

Corn tortillas, for serving

2 red radishes, sliced paper thin, for garnish

3 limes, cut into wedges, for garnish

Ropa Vieja

This is going to be the easiest and tastiest ropa vieja that you will ever eat. This is one of my girlfriends' favorite dishes to make because of how easy it is. Why go to a Cuban restaurant when you can have your own personal restaurant at home?

Serves 4 to 6

This can be prepared in the oven or a slow cooker.

Oven method: Preheat your oven to 275°F (140°C). Heat a Dutch oven over medium heat on your stovetop. Season the meat with the salt on both sides, then sear on both sides, 2 to 3 minutes per side.

Add all the remaining ingredients—that's right, you read correctly—we're one-pot cooking here! Cover, place in the oven and forget about it for 5 hours. Check at the 5-hour mark to see whether the meat is tender. If it needs more time, cook for another 15 minutes. The meat should pull apart with just a fork.

Slow cooker method: Season and sear the meat on all sides in a large sauté pan, then transfer to a 6- to 8-quart (5.7- to 7.6-L) slow cooker along with the rest of the ingredients. Cook for 5 hours on the LOW setting, or until fork-tender.

Goes well with rice and Cuban Black Beans (page 112).

1½ lb (680 g) flank steak, London broil or chuck

1 tbsp (18 g) salt

2 (8-oz [227-g]) cans tomato sauce

1 red bell pepper, seeded and julienned

1 green bell pepper, seeded and julienned

1 onion, julienned

1 bunch cilantro, chopped

¼ cup (60 ml) red cooking wine

1 tsp ground cumin

1 tbsp (7 g) paprika

1 tbsp (7 g) onion powder

1 tbsp (9 g) garlic powder

1 bay leaf

¼ cup (60 ml) olive brine

8 olives (optional)

3 red potatoes, large diced

2 tbsp (30 ml) olive oil

Take That Chicken and
Throw It on Top of a Beer

Who doesn't like beer? Especially when you have a chicken sitting on a beer. What could go wrong? Nothing! I love this dish because you get to put it on the barbecue, cover it and walk away. Play some activities outside, drink some beer, drink some beer and drink some beer. Let your chicken cook slow and low while you drink the remaining five beers. If you don't drink beer, soda pop would work. Using soda pop will give a sweeter taste to the dish.

Serves 4 to 6

Preheat your barbecue grill. You want a temperature of 225°F (110°C) for the bird to cook. Slow and low.

In a small bowl, combine the garlic powder, onion powder, paprika, white pepper and salt. Add the butter and make a paste of the mixture. Rub the paste all over the chicken, including inside and underneath the skin, until the paste is used up. Place the rosemary and thyme inside the chicken.

Pour one-quarter of the beer (1½ cans) into a disposable aluminum foil pan. Put an empty beer can in the middle of the pan and place your chicken—standing up, legs down, wings up—over the beer can all the way through to the bottom. Close the lid of the grill and don't worry about it for 5 hours, though you can baste it halfway through the cooking time, if you like. I prefer to baste twice. Just remember, the more you open the lid, the more heat you will let out. Drink the remaining beer or soda pop while the chicken cooks.

Take the chicken from the grill and remove the beer can. Let the chicken rest for 10 minutes on a plate. Remove the legs, wings and thighs. Cut the breast off the bone and slice.

Goes great with Sweet and Spicy Baked Beans (page 115).

1½ tsp (5 g) garlic powder

1½ tsp (4 g) onion powder

1½ tsp (4 g) smoked paprika

1 tsp ground white pepper

2 tsp (13 g) kosher salt

2 tbsp (28 g) unsalted butter, at room temperature

1 (4- to 5-lb [1.8- to 2.3-kg]) chicken

2 sprigs rosemary

2 sprigs thyme

6 (12-oz [355-ml]) cans beer of your choice (I recommend a nice lager) or your preferred flavor soda pop, divided

The Best Dinner *Ideas*

There is nothing more satisfying than cooking all day and eating the finished product. This is why dinner is considered the main meal of the day in low and slow cooking—you work on it all day and then savor what you've made.

The recipes in this chapter are dear to my heart. They will become some of your favorite treasures, too. I put together a collection of memorable meals I have had around the world—the ones that really inspire.

Standout Pork Shank *with Broccoli and Brussels Sprout Slaw*

The shank is located on the pig between the ham and the hock. Some shanks are described as ham hocks. Don't be confused; for this recipe, we require the cut below the ham on the leg. If you never had pork shank before . . . I am sorry. Once you try this recipe, you might be having shank once a week. You will get notes of sweet and spicy with a bit of tang. The meat is going to be fork tender and fall off the bone.

Serves 4

Preheat your oven to 225°F (110°C).

Heat a Dutch oven over medium to high heat for 5 minutes. Meanwhile, in a small bowl, combine the brown sugar, salt, cayenne, black pepper and rosemary and mix until well incorporated. Evenly distribute on all 4 pork shanks.

Dredge your shanks with the flour, making sure you shake off any excess.

Add the oil to the pot and, working in batches so you don't overcrowd the pan, sear the shanks on all sides. It'll be 10 minutes per batch, 5 minutes per side. Remove the shanks and set aside on a plate. Add your onion to the pot and cook until translucent, about 3 minutes. Add your garlic and sauté for another 2 minutes. Deglaze the pot with the white wine, making sure to scrape the bottom. Bring to a quick boil, then add your vegetable stock, bay leaves, tomato paste and cider vinegar. Give a quick stir. Return the pork shanks to the pot. Cover and set in the middle of the oven. Cook for 7 hours.

(Continued)

Pork Shank

¼ cup (60 g) light brown sugar

1½ tbsp (28 g) kosher salt

1 tsp cayenne pepper

1 tbsp (6 g) freshly ground black pepper

1 tbsp (3 g) dried rosemary

4 fresh pork foreshanks

½ cup (60 g) all-purpose flour

2 tbsp (30 ml) canola oil

1 yellow onion, sliced thinly

4 cloves garlic, smashed

1 cup (240 ml) white wine

1 cup (240 ml) vegetable broth (homemade [page 137] or store-bought)

3 bay leaves

1 tsp tomato paste

2 tbsp (30 ml) cider vinegar

Standout Pork Shank . . .
continued

While the pork is cooking, start your broccoli and Brussels slaw: Remove the stalk from the broccoli head and set the rest of the broccoli aside. Trim and clean the stalk, then cut it into thin planks and then into fine strips. Trim and clean the Brussels sprouts as well. Shave the Brussels sprouts and the reserved broccoli head with a knife; it will be easier if you use a mandoline. In a bowl, combine the shaved sprouts and broccoli with the broccoli stalk strips and set aside.

In another bowl, whisk together the lemon juice, olive oil, mustard, black pepper and salt, then add the Parmesan cheese and walnuts. Evenly distribute the lemon juice mixture over the shredded slaw. Lightly toss and then keep covered in the refrigerator. Pull out 30 minutes prior to dinner and top with the blue cheese crumbles.

Remove the shanks from the oven and strain the juices into a pot. Bring to a boil and reduce by half. Serve by pouring the sauce over the pork with the slaw on the side.

Broccoli and Brussels Sprout Slaw

1 large head broccoli

8 oz (225 g) fresh Brussels sprouts

Juice of 2 lemons

1 cup (240 ml) olive oil

1 tsp whole-grain mustard

1 tsp freshly ground black pepper

1 tsp salt

4 oz (115 g) Parmesan cheese, shaved

4 oz (115 g) toasted walnuts

1 oz (28 g) blue cheese crumbles

Cassoulet, My Way

There are many renditions of a cassoulet. This dish is one of the first recipes I learned when I was in a French culinary school, where I learned how to make it the traditional Languedoc way. But over the years, I have come across several different varieties of this classic dish. It gets its name from the vessel it is cooked in, a *cassole*. This recipe takes all day to build the flavors, since they are layered. It's loaded with fatty sausage, ham hock, salt pork; and the freshness from the thyme and oregano gives this dish a nice fresh touch. This cassoulet does not call for duck confit, but you can add it if you like.

Serves 4 to 6

The night before, in a bowl, cover the beans with 3 inches (8 cm) of water and let sit overnight.

Preheat your oven to 300°F (150°C) and make sure the rack is in the center. Heat a Dutch oven over medium-high heat and add the olive oil.

Add your salt pork and cook until golden on all sides, about 3 minutes per side, then remove from the pot and set aside in a bowl. Drain away all but 2 tablespoons (30 ml) of fat from the pot. Add your sausages and sear on all sides until golden brown, about 3 minutes, making sure you are constantly moving them around. Remove the sausages and set aside with the salt pork. Sear your ham hock on all sides for 4 minutes per side, then remove and set aside. Season your chicken heavily with salt and pepper. Sear it on both sides until golden brown, 3 to 4 minutes per side. Remove the chicken from the pot and set aside. Drain the soaked beans.

Add your onion, carrot and celery to the pot, making sure you're scraping the bottom of the pot to get everything off. Next, deglaze the pot with the white wine. Add the tomato, chicken stock, cloves, bay leaves, garlic, thyme, oregano and drained beans. Bring to a simmer and cover. Lower the heat and cook for 50 minutes. You want the beans to be tender but still have a bite to them. Using tongs, remove the cloves and bay leaves from the pot. Return the sausages, salt pork, ham hock and chicken to the pot. Give a stir to incorporate everything, making sure the chicken is skin side up on top of the beans.

(Continued)

1 lb (455 g) dried cannellini beans

1 tbsp (15 ml) olive oil

8 oz (225 g) salt pork, cut into ½" (1.3-cm) cubes

1 lb (455 g) pork sausages

1 fresh ham hock

4 chicken leg quarters

Salt and freshly ground black pepper

1 onion, chopped

1 carrot, chopped

2 ribs celery, chopped

1 cup (240 ml) white wine

1 large tomato, chopped

2 cups (475 ml) chicken stock (homemade [page 136] or store-bought)

4 whole cloves

2 bay leaves

8 cloves garlic, smashed

3 sprigs thyme

3 sprigs fresh oregano

2 cups (230 g) bread crumbs

2 tbsp (8 g) chopped fresh parsley

Cassoulet, My Way
continued

In a bowl, mix together the bread crumbs and parsley. Spread this mixture evenly over the chicken.

Transfer the pot to the oven and cook, uncovered, until a crust forms, about 2 hours, adding water if necessary to keep the beans submerged: Poke a hole along an edge of the top crust with a spoon and carefully pour in the water.

Place back in the oven and continue to cook, making sure you break the crust every 45 minutes until the 5-hour mark is reached.

After 5 hours, the crust will be brown. Remove from the oven and serve immediately.

Rich and Velvety Coq au Vin

I remember it as if it was yesterday; I was in my international cuisine class in culinary school and we were given recipes and told to follow them. My recipe was, of course, for coq au vin. So, what can be so bad about that? Well . . . when it came time to make the roux, you need equal parts of flour and fat and I didn't realize. My dish looked like a thick porridge. Epic fail. Not this recipe! The end result will be a rich and velvety sauce that has you coming back for more.

Serves 4

Preheat your oven to 225°F (110°C). Heat a large cast-iron skillet or Dutch oven over medium heat. Add your olive oil and stir in your pancetta. Cook until the pancetta starts to crisp up, about 5 minutes. Remove from the pot and reserve on a paper towel–lined plate.

Season the chicken legs and thighs with salt and pepper. Put the chicken legs in the pot first and brown on all sides, 3 to 4 minutes per side. Remove the legs from the pot and set aside on a plate. Repeat the same process for the thighs.

Add the onion and carrot to the pot and sauté until the onion is translucent, about 3 minutes. Add the garlic and mushrooms. If you need to add more oil, add up to 1 tablespoon (15 ml). Add your brandy and scrape all the yumminess off the bottom of the pot. Return the chicken and pancetta to the pot and add any juices left behind as well.

Pour in your wine and chicken stock. Add your thyme and bring to a quick boil. Cover and put in the oven. Cook for 6 hours 30 minutes.

In a small bowl, mix together the flour and butter. Remove the pot from the oven and place over medium-low heat. Add the flour mixture and let thicken, 3 to 5 minutes.

Season with salt and pepper, if needed.

1 tbsp (15 ml) olive oil, plus more if needed

3 oz (170 g) pancetta, cut into strips

4 chicken legs, skin on

4 chicken thighs, skin on

1 tbsp (18 g) salt, plus more for serving, if needed

1 tbsp (6 g) freshly ground pepper, plus more for serving, if needed

1 white onion, diced

1 carrot, diced

2 cloves garlic, minced

2 cups (140 g) thickly sliced button mushrooms

½ cup (120 ml) brandy

½ (750-ml) bottle red wine, your favorite variety (I like a merlot)

1½ cups (355 ml) chicken stock (homemade [page 136] or store-bought)

6 sprigs thyme

2 tbsp (15 g) all-purpose flour

1 tbsp (14 g) unsalted butter, room temperature

The Best Indoor Brisket

Who doesn't love a great brisket? I had a five-hour layover in Texas and I was determined to have some amazing barbecue. Everyone in Texas smokes their brisket. I saw some huge smokers! But this one little hut I found didn't have a smoker. They slow roasted their brisket in the oven instead of a smoker, so it eliminated that red smoke ring you usually get when smoking. With my seasonings and the slow and low technique . . . get ready for there to be no leftovers.

Serves 6

Preheat your oven to 225°F (110°C).

In a bowl, combine the garlic, chili powder, onion powder, brown sugar, salt, black pepper, dry mustard and smoked paprika and use the mixture to season the brisket on both sides, making sure you pat, not rub, it on. Place the brisket in a roasting pan and set aside to come to room temperature, about 1 hour.

In a large sauté pan, heat the vegetable oil over medium heat. Sear the brisket on all sides until golden brown, 5 to 6 minutes total. Place back in the roasting pan. Deglaze the bottom of the sauté pan with ¼ cup (60 ml) of the beef stock, then add that mixture and the remaining beef stock to the roasting pan. Place the roasting pan on the center rack of the oven. Cook for 7 hours, or until fork-tender.

Remove the brisket from the roasting pan and let rest for 20 to 30 minutes before serving.

This goes great with the barbecue sauce recipe on page 139.

2 tbsp (18 g) granulated garlic

2 tbsp (15 g) dark chili powder

1 tbsp (7 g) onion powder

1 tbsp (15 g) light brown sugar

3 tbsp (54 g) salt

1 tbsp (6 g) freshly ground black pepper

1 tsp dry mustard

1 tsp smoked paprika

1 (4- to 5-lb [1.8- to 2.3-kg]) beef brisket, trimmed

¼ cup (60 ml) vegetable oil

2 cups (475 ml) beef stock (homemade [page 134] or store-bought), divided

Citrus-Smoked Salmon

Salmon is always amazing, but nothing beats smoked salmon, in my opinion. Cured and smoked salmon together is a home run. You can use the leftovers for breakfast in an omelet or on some crackers with a schmear. This can keep for seven days refrigerated if wrapped properly in a plastic wrap. Or even better—vacuum seal it.

Serves 6

In a medium-sized bowl, combine the salt, sugar, peppercorns, coriander seeds, fennel seeds and lemon, lime and orange zest. In a separate bowl, combine and reserve the citrus juices for brushing.

Select a baking sheet that is the same size as the fish and line it with aluminum foil. Pour a third of the salt mixture onto the prepared pan and spread it out evenly. Place the fish, skin side down, over the mixture in the pan. Spread the remaining salt mixture on top of the fish, making sure you evenly coat the fish with the mixture.

Cover the fish with aluminum foil and crimp the sides and ends of the foil together to seal in the fish. Cure for 12 hours to 3 days in the refrigerator.

Heat your smoker to 225°F (110°C).

Remove the fish from the foil and rinse both sides to make sure all of the curing mixture is off. Pat the fish dry.

Drizzle the oil on the skin side of the fish. Put the fish, skin side down, on the cedar wood. Brush the reserved orange, lemon and lime juice mixture on the flesh side of the fish. Put the wood and fish into the smoker and smoke for 1 hour. The fish is already cooked from the cure; we are just adding the flavor of the smoke to finish it off. When the hour is up, remove the fish from the smoker.

Time to enjoy. Using a sharp knife at a 30-degree angle, cut the fish into thin slices.

1 cup (300 g) kosher salt

½ cup (100 g) sugar

1 tsp black peppercorns

1 tsp coriander seeds

1 tsp fennel seeds

Zest and juice of 1 lemon

Zest and juice of 1 lime

Zest and juice of 1 orange

2 lb (905 g) salmon fillet, skin on

1 tbsp (15 m) olive oil

1 (4 x 6" [10 x 15–cm]) uncured cedar slab, soaked in cold water for 1 hour

Chicken Chasseur

This is another French classic that is great for any dinner get-together. Your guests will rave about how amazing the meal is and think that you have cooked over the stove for hours.

Chasseur is also known as hunter's sauce, which is a simple brown sauce that consists of mushrooms and tomatoes. I like the saltiness and the smoky flavor from the bacon.

Serves 4 to 6

Season the chicken heavily on all sides with the salt and pepper, then dredge the front and back of the chicken with the flour, making sure you shake off any excess.

Preheat your oven to 225°F (110°C). Meanwhile, heat a Dutch oven over medium heat for 5 minutes, then add the olive oil. Add your bacon and cook until it's three-quarters of the way cooked, about 4 minutes. Remove the bacon from the pan and set aside. In batches, trying not to overcrowd the Dutch oven, sear the chicken on all sides, 2 minutes per side. When you are on your last batch add the 2 tablespoons (28 g) of butter.

Remove the chicken from the pot and add the mushrooms and shallots. Cook, giving a nice caramelization to the shallots, 2 to 3 minutes, then add the white wine and deglaze the pan, making sure you scrape the bottom of the pan. Add your chicken stock, tomato paste and tomatoes and return the bacon and chicken to the pot. Let come to a boil, remove from the heat, cover and put in the oven. Cook for 6 hours 30 minutes. Remove from the oven and let settle for 15 minutes before serving. Garnish with the fresh parsley and thyme.

This goes great with mashed potatoes.

1 (2½- to 4-lb [1.1- to 1.8-kg]) chicken, cut into 8 pieces: legs, thighs, breasts and wings

2 tbsp (24 g) combined salt and freshly ground black pepper

1⅓ cups (170 g) all-purpose flour

2 tbsp (30 ml) olive oil

2 slices bacon, cut into thin strips

2 tbsp (28 g) unsalted butter, at room temperature

4 oz (115 g) button mushrooms, sliced

2 shallots, sliced

½ cup (120 ml) white wine

2 cups (475 ml) chicken stock (homemade [page 136] or store-bought)

1 tbsp (16 g) tomato paste

2 tomatoes, seeded and diced

½ cup (28 oz) finely chopped fresh flat-leaf parsley

3½ tbsp (14 g) finely chopped fresh thyme

Nothing Baby about These Ribs
with Burrata and Peach Salad

These ribs will fall off the bone and be finger-lickin' good. They have a flavorful dry rub that mimics a dried Texas barbecue rub, with a few extra spices to kick it up a notch. You can keep the extra seasoning in an airtight container for another use. Store in a dry area. For the salad, if you really want to get the best flavor, I would suggest grilling the peaches on both sides. That nice char mark on the peaches gives it this nice bitter taste that goes perfectly with the sweetness of the fruit and creaminess of the burrata.

Serves 4 to 6

For the ribs, preheat your grill and maintain a temperature of 225°F (110°C). In the meantime, place the ribs, bone side up, on a cutting board. Slide your fingers between the membrane and the bones. Once the membrane pulls apart and you have a good grip, pull it off in one swoop.

In a bowl, stir together the remaining ingredients, except the barbecue sauce, to make a rub. Pat a good amount of the mixture on the ribs to coat on all sides, making sure not to rub the mixture on. Place the ribs over indirect heat and cook for 6 hours, making sure the grill stays at 225°F (110°C). At the 6-hour mark, grab a bone and give it a wiggle. If the bone pulls apart from the meat, the ribs are done. If not, be ready to check again in 15 minutes.

Baste the ribs on both sides with the barbecue sauce. Kick up the grill to 300°F (150°C) and flip the ribs every 10 minutes for the next 30 minutes, basting while you're flipping. Let the ribs rest for 10 minutes before cutting.

(Continued)

Ribs

2 racks baby back ribs

½ cup (115 g) light brown sugar

1 tbsp (7 g) smoked paprika

2 tsp (4 g) cayenne pepper

1 tsp freshly ground black pepper

1 tsp ground white pepper

2 tbsp (18 g) garlic powder

1 tbsp (7 g) onion powder

1 tbsp (9 g) dry mustard

½ tsp ground cumin

1 tsp ground coriander

¼ cup (60 g) kosher salt

1 tbsp (8 g) dark chili powder

Your favorite barbecue sauce

Nothing Baby about These Ribs
continued

Prepare the dressing: In a small bowl, combine your lemon juice, mustard and sugar. Slowly drizzle in the olive oil while whisking vigorously to emulsify the dressing. When finished, set aside.

Prepare the salad: Place the arugula in a large bowl, add the dressing and toss. Transfer to the center of a large plate. Arrange the peaches going in a circle around or on the arugula, all facing the same direction, leaving room between each slice. In between the peach slices, put a piece of burrata. Sprinkle the olive oil on the peaches and burrata, then drizzle with the balsamic glaze. Season with salt and pepper to taste.

Serve the ribs with the salad.

Dressing

1 tbsp (15 ml) fresh lemon juice

1 tsp whole-grain mustard

½ tsp sugar

¼ cup (60 ml) olive oil

Salad

8 oz (225 g) baby arugula

6 peaches, sliced into ½" (1.3-cm) slices along the pit into half-moon shapes

8 oz (225 g) burrata, drained on a paper towel, then sliced into eighths right before plating

2 tbsp (30 ml) olive oil

3 tbsp (45 ml) balsamic glaze

Salt and freshly ground black pepper

Smoked Ham Shank
with Watermelon Relish

In this recipe, you will basically be making your own ham without the brine, by just smoking it. It takes between 6 and 7 hours for a 10- to 12-pound (4.5- to 5.4-kg) ham. The meat will be so tender that it will pull away from the bone. This can be done with a smoker or on a grill. The relish is a great pair to this smoky ham.

Serves 6 to 8

Prepare the ham: Preheat your grill to 225°F (110°C). Use aluminum foil to make a pocket by folding the foil in half and then folding each side inward. Place your wood chips inside the pocket and close by folding the foil up. Poke a hole in the top and bottom and place on the direct heat of the grill. When the wood chips are smoking, about 10 minutes, shut off one side of the grill and place your foil pocket on the off side of the grill.

In a spray bottle, combine the apple juice and maple syrup. Give the mixture a shake and spray a nice amount on the ham. Reserve the rest of the mixture; you will be using it to baste the ham during the cooking process.

In a bowl, mix together the paprika, granulated garlic, onion powder, cayenne pepper, dry mustard, brown sugar and salt, then rub an even amount all over the ham.

Place your ham on the off side as well, setting an empty pan under the ham to catch any drippings. Let smoke for 2 hours. Lift the lid and give the ham a generous spray of the apple juice mixture. Close the lid and repeat this at the 4-hour mark. Check the ham at 6 hours 30 minutes. Its internal temperature should be 160 to 170°F (71 to 77°C). Let rest for 15 minutes before serving.

(Continued)

Smoked Ham

2 cups (180 g) wood chips (I like cherry), soaked for 30 minutes, then drained

2 cups (475 ml) apple juice

1 cup (240 ml) pure maple syrup

1 fresh (10- to 12-lb [4.5- to 5.4-kg]) shank portion fresh ham

2 tbsp (14 g) sweet paprika

2 tbsp (18 g) granulated garlic

1 tbsp (7 g) onion powder

1½ tsp (3 g) cayenne pepper

1½ tsp (5 g) dry mustard

½ cup (115 g) light brown sugar

2 tbsp (36 g) salt

Smoked Ham Shank *with Watermelon Relish* *continued*

Prepare the relish: In a medium-sized bowl, stir together the watermelon, jalapeños, basil, mint, shallot, white wine vinegar, virgin olive oil and kosher salt. Chill for 10 minutes before serving.

Remove the bone from the ham then top it with the relish or keep the relish in the bowl and serve it on the side.

Watermelon Relish

2 cups (300 g) finely chopped watermelon

2 jalapeño peppers, seeded and finely chopped

2 tbsp (5 g) finely chopped fresh basil

2 tbsp (12 g) finely chopped fresh mint

3 tbsp (28 g) minced shallot

1 tbsp (15 ml) white wine vinegar

1 tbsp (15 ml) virgin olive oil

1 tsp kosher salt

Pork Belly This

Baconnnnnn . . . In 20-plus years in the restaurant industry, you come across so many different ways to make pork belly, from sous viding to roasting to slicing and baking. My favorite way is actually roasting, which traps the flavor. The pork belly is crisp on the outside with juicy, moist, tender meat on the inside . . . pure yum!

Serves 4

Preheat your oven to 200°F (90°C). Lightly score your pork belly; that's making gentle slices using the tip of your knife at a diagonal across the top of the belly.

In a small bowl, combine the salt, garlic powder, smoked paprika, cayenne, cinnamon and cumin. Rub the mixture evenly on the top and bottom of the belly. Wrap the belly in plastic wrap and then in foil, twice. Place the wrapped belly in a roasting pan and cook for 6 hours, then check the tenderness. If the pork belly still needs more time to become fork-tender, cook for another 30 minutes to an hour.

Remove the pork belly from the oven and let it cool in its wrappings for 2 hours. Place, still wrapped, in the refrigerator and chill for 6 to 10 hours. It is best to let chill overnight.

Remove the pork from the fridge and unwrap it. Cut it into 1-inch (2.5-cm) strips, then into 1-inch (2.5-cm) cubes. In a medium-size to large sauté pan, heat ¼ cup (60 ml) of the oil over medium heat. Wait 6 minutes, make sure the oil is hot, then sauté the cubed pork in batches for 3 to 4 minutes per side, or until golden brown, adding more oil as needed for each subsequent batch. Remove from the oil and season to taste with salt and black pepper. Serve with tortillas (if using).

1½ lb (680 g) pork belly, skin removed

1½ tsp (9 g) kosher salt

1¼ tsp (3 g) garlic powder

1¼ tsp (3 g) smoked paprika

1 tsp cayenne pepper

¼ tsp ground cinnamon

¼ tsp ground cumin

½ cup (120 ml) canola oil, divided

Salt and freshly ground black pepper

Tortillas, to serve (optional)

Slow-Roasted Cod *with Chimichurri*

This recipe is so easy that it will become one of your star dishes. The fresh cod will be flaky and moist, while the chimichurri sauce will give it a nice kick at the end. Slow roasting is the key to keeping the cod moist.

Serves 6

Preheat your oven to 225°F (110°C).

In a food processor, combine the garlic, chile, red pepper flakes, parsley, cilantro and scallions. I want you to say it with me as you put your finger on the pulse button. Pulse. Pulse. Pulse. Pulsssssseeeeee (counting to 4). Pulse. Transfer the mixture to a bowl. Add the lemon zest and juice, 1 teaspoon of the salt and ¼ cup (60 ml) of the olive oil. Place in the refrigerator to chill.

With nonstick spray, spray a roasting pan large enough to fit the fish. Place the fish in the pan, skin side down. Let it come to room temperature. Drizzle the fish with 1 tablespoon (15 ml) of the oil. Season with the remaining 1½ teaspoons (9 g) of the salt and the black pepper. In a bowl, toss the tomatoes with the remaining tablespoon (15 ml) of oil. Place the tomatoes around the fish. Put the pan in the middle of the oven and cook for 2 hours, or until flaky.

Top the cod with the chimichurri before serving. This goes great with Cuban Black Beans (page 112).

2 cloves garlic, smashed

1 Fresno chile, seeded and chopped

½ tsp red pepper flakes

½ bunch parsley

½ bunch cilantro

5 scallions, diced

Zest and juice of 1 lemon

2½ tsp (15 g) salt, divided

6 tbsp (90 ml) olive oil, divided

Nonstick spray

2 lb (905 g) black cod fillet, skin-on

1 tsp freshly ground black pepper

1 pint (178 g) cherry tomatoes

Slow-Roasted Pork Butt
with Sweet & Spicy Glaze

While visiting the island of Jamaica, I fell in love with its cuisine and their passion for food. One of the best things I had was this sweet and spicy pork butt. It had a certain crunch to it, with a sweet, sticky glaze. So I had to recreate it. My favorite way to eat this pork is with homemade corn tortillas.

Serves 6 to 8

In a bowl, stir together the granulated garlic, paprika, onion powder, cayenne, black pepper, cinnamon and brown sugar. Use the mixture to evenly coat the pork butt, making sure you pat, not rub, it on. Rubbing clogs the pores of the meat, whereas patting helps it breathe. Put the pork butt on a plate and let it chill, covered, in the refrigerator for 8 hours. The longer you let it sit, the more flavor you will get out of the pork.

Preheat your oven to 250°F (120°C).

In a small saucepan, combine the maple syrup, jalapeño and Dr Pepper. Bring to a boil and let simmer for 4 minutes.

Meanwhile heat a large sauté pan or Dutch oven over medium-high heat until hot. When the pan is hot, add the oil. Sear the pork butt until golden brown on all sides, 5 minutes per side.

When the oven is at temperature, put the pork in a casserole dish or keep in the Dutch oven. Glaze the pork with the syrup mixture and cover. Let the pork cook for 1 hour, remove from the oven and glaze the pork again with the syrup mixture. Continue to do this every hour until the pork is fork tender; 6 to 8 hours is the average time.

Remove from the oven and let rest for 15 minutes before serving.

2 tbsp (18 g) granulated garlic

2 tbsp (14 g) paprika

2 tbsp (14 g) onion powder

2 tbsp (11 g) cayenne pepper

1 tbsp (6 g) freshly ground black pepper

1 tbsp (7 g) ground cinnamon

1 tbsp (15 g) light brown sugar

1 (3-lb [1.4-kg]) pork butt

1 cup (240 ml) pure maple syrup

1 jalapeño pepper, seeded and sliced in half

1 (12-oz [355-ml]) can Dr Pepper

3 tbsp (45 ml) vegetable oil

Slow-Smoked Beef Ribs

When I think of beef ribs, I think of the Flintstones. Yabba dabba doo. For this recipe, you want to use chuck ribs. They're usually sold as a plate of four, meaning four bones. This is a set-and-forget recipe. Barbecue is not about the cooking time, but more about the touch and internal temperature. Here, you're gonna have the natural flavors of the ribs stand out with the use of heavy salt. It will make a nice crust with a tender juicy inside.

Serves 4

Preheat your smoker to 275°F (140°C). Alternatively, preheat your oven to 225°F (110°C).

If your beef ribs still have a fat cap, you want to trim that off—remove everything, even the silver skin. If you weren't smoking the ribs, you'd leave the fat cap on and score it. While roasting it would become a nice bubbly crust. But that's another day, another recipe.

Heavily season the beef ribs with the salt and pepper in a 3-to-1 ratio (I start with 3 ounces of salt and 1 ounce of black pepper). Tap the salt into the meat. Don't rub. Tap. Tap.

To cook in a smoker, place the meat in the center of the smoker rack, bone side down. In a spray bottle, combine the water and cider vinegar. Once the beef has been cooking for at least 2 hours, lift up the lid and spray the beef with the vinegar mixture, then repeat every hour and a half. You want to cook the ribs until all the thickest part of the meat reads 210°F (99°C), making sure you do not touch the bone while checking the temperature. You can also check whether they're done by seeing whether you can move the bones away from the meat. Cook for 6 to 8 hours total.

To cook in the oven, place in the oven and cook for 6 hours without turning over or rotating the ribs, and test for doneness as described above.

Remove the ribs from the smoker or oven and place on a cutting board. Wrap the meat in uncoated butcher's paper and let rest for at least 1 hour.

Once done resting, slice the ribs in between each bone.

This goes great with Southern Collard Greens (page 116).

1 (4-bone) plate beef chuck ribs

Kosher salt

Freshly ground black pepper

½ cup (120 ml) water

1 cup (240 ml) cider vinegar

Soy-Marinated Short Ribs
with Asian Slaw

This is one of my favorite summer dishes. The marinade will make your taste buds explode. Even though short ribs tend to be on the heavier side, the fresh vegetables from the Asian slaw brighten up this dish. Set and forget!

Serves 4

Prepare the short ribs: In a bowl, whisk together the soy sauce, brown sugar, rice vinegar, hoisin sauce, sesame oil, garlic, ginger, red pepper flakes, lime juice, shallot and 1 cup (240 ml) of the water. Place the short ribs in a large ziplock bag and pour the mixture over them. Cover and marinate the ribs in the refrigerator for 8 to 10 hours, or for the best result, overnight.

Remove the short ribs from the refrigerator 1 hour prior to cooking, to get the chill off. Remove the ribs from the marinade and pat dry. Strain the marinade into a pot and add the remaining 2 cups (475 ml) of water. Bring to a boil over high heat.

Meanwhile, preheat your Dutch oven over medium-high heat and add the oil. When the oil looks like it is spreading around the pan, sear the short ribs on all sides until golden brown; you want to have a nice sear, so give them 4 to 5 minutes per side. When the marinade has come to a boil, pour it over the short ribs and cover the pot. Lower the heat to low and cook for 2 hours. Uncover, spoon the marinade over the short ribs and cook, covered, for another 2 to 3 hours, or until tender.

(Continued)

Short Ribs

¾ cup (175 ml) low-sodium soy sauce

½ cup (115 g) packed light brown sugar

½ cup (120 ml) unseasoned rice vinegar

½ cup (120 ml) hoisin sauce

2 tbsp (30 ml) sesame oil (toasted or not)

2 tbsp (20 g) minced garlic

2 tbsp (16 g) peeled and grated fresh ginger

1 tsp red pepper flakes

Juice of 1 lime

1 shallot, diced

3 cups (710 ml) water, divided

3 lb (1.4 kg) bone-in short ribs, 2 to 3" (5 to 7.5 cm) long

3 tbsp (45 ml) olive oil

Soy-Marinated Short Ribs *with Asian Slaw* *continued*

While the short ribs are cooking, you can get your slaw together; alternatively, the slaw can also be made a day in advance. In a bowl, combine the broccoli stalk, carrots, bok choy, green and red cabbage, bell peppers and jalapeño in a bowl. Mix together thoroughly. Cover and store in the refrigerator until needed. When ready to serve, in a small bowl, whisk together the scallions, cilantro, soy sauce, rice vinegar, sesame oil, sugar and red pepper flakes to make a dressing.

When the short ribs are done, using a spoon—a slotted spoon would be best—remove them from the pot and place on a cutting board. For the best result, try to skim as much of the fat off the sauce as possible. Increase the heat to medium and let the sauce reduce by one-quarter. If the sauce can coat the back of a spoon, it is ready. Return the short ribs to their pot and evenly coat the ribs with the sauce. I like to do this in the Dutch oven because it is less messy than doing it on the cutting board

To serve, add the dressing to the slaw and toss. Put the short ribs in a bowl and top with the slaw. This tastes great with steamed jasmine rice as an additional side.

Asian Slaw

1 broccoli stalk, thinly sliced (reserve florets for another purpose)

2 carrots, peeled and thinly sliced

½ head bok choy, thinly sliced

¼ head green cabbage, thinly sliced

¼ head red cabbage, thinly sliced

1 red bell pepper, thinly sliced

1 orange bell pepper, thinly sliced

1 jalapeño pepper, thinly sliced

2 scallions, thinly sliced

1 bunch cilantro, minced

¼ cup (60 ml) soy sauce

¼ cup (60 ml) rice vinegar

¼ cup (60 ml) toasted sesame oil

2 tbsp (26 g) sugar

1 tbsp (4 g) red pepper flakes

Sausage & Gravy Pizza

Sausage and gravy pizza—yes, please. This recipe works the best if everything is made the day before. If you can do that, then it will be well worth the wait. I love making my homemade pizza, there is some kind of gratification that goes along with it. Don't forget to throw the pizza in the air when making your dough, just like in the pizzerias.

Serves 4

Prepare the sausage: Preheat a Dutch oven or large sauté pan over medium heat. Add the butter, then add your onion and cook until translucent, 3 to 4 minutes. Add your sausage meat and rosemary and start browning. You want to cook the sausage meat fully, 8 to 10 minutes. Now, sprinkle the flour all over the sausage mixture. Fully incorporate by stirring the mixture constantly. When the flour starts to have a nutty smell, you want to add your milk, garlic powder and salt. Whisk, whisk, whisk. Pour your mixture into a slow cooker, set to LOW and cook for 4 hours.

While the sausage mixture is cooking, get your pizza dough together: In the bowl of an electric mixer, mix together 1 cup (125 g) of the flour with the yeast, salt and sugar. If you don't have a stand mixer, use a large bowl and a wooden spoon.

Add the olive oil and warm water. Using the hook attachment, begin to mix on a low setting. Add another cup (125 g) of the flour and incorporate. Increase the mixer speed to medium and mix until the dough forms a ball and is pulling off the sides of the bowl, adding additional flour as needed to keep it from sticking.

Lightly brush a clean bowl with some of the olive oil. Lightly flour your hands and remove the dough mixture from its mixing bowl. Form the dough into a ball and place it in the oiled bowl. Cover the bowl with plastic wrap and put in a warm spot to rise. Allow the dough to double in size, 40 minutes to an hour.

Once the dough has risen, gently deflate, using your hands. Knead for 3 to 5 minutes.

(Continued)

Sausage

2 tbsp (28 g) unsalted butter

½ yellow onion, diced

1 lb (455 g) pork sausage meat, ground

1 tsp dried rosemary

⅓ cup (41 g) all-purpose flour

3 cups (710 ml) milk

1 tsp garlic powder

1 tsp salt

Pizza Dough

2½ cups (313 g) all-purpose flour, divided

1 (¼-oz [8-g]) packet dry active yeast

1 tsp salt

2 tsp (8 g) sugar

3 tbsp (45 ml) olive oil, plus more for the bowl

¼ cup (60 ml) water, warmed to 110°F (43°C)

Sausage & Gravy Pizza
continued

Preheat your oven to 425°F (220°C).

Gently dust the counter with flour and place the dough in the center. Using a rolling pin, roll out to a 12-inch (31.5-cm)-diameter round that is ⅛ inch (3 mm) thick. Gently pinch the edges to form a crust.

Place the pizza dough on a parchment-lined pizza pan, or if you have a ceramic round for making pizza, use that.

Brush the pizza dough with 1 tablespoon (15 ml) of oil. Add your sausage mixture. Make 4 little divots in the sausage mixture. Break 1 egg into each divot.

Place the pizza in the center of the oven and bake for 13 to 15 minutes. Garnish with the sliced scallions, drizzle with olive oil and sprinkle with black pepper.

4 large eggs, to build pizza

Scallions, thinly sliced on an angle, for garnish

1 tbsp (15 ml) olive oil, plus more for garnish

1½ tsp (3 g) freshly ground black pepper

Set-and-Forget It Quiche

This is another lifesaver meal. If you know you are going to have a late night, you can start this right before you go to bed, and by the time you wake up in the morning, it will be finished just like that. This is one of the first recipes I learned in culinary school. You will have it memorized in no time and have your friends thinking you're a classically trained chef.

Serves 6 to 8

Make sure you butter the inside of a 6- to 8-quart (5.7- to 7.6-L) slow cooker. Also give it a spray of nonstick spray. Set aside.

In a medium-sized sauté pan, cook your sliced sausage links over medium heat, 4 to 5 minutes. Drain and set aside.

In a large bowl, whisk your eggs with the milk. Add the spinach, goat cheese and cheddar cheese, plus the sausages, to the bowl. Season with the salt and pepper. Pour the mixture into the slow cooker and sprinkle the Parmesan cheese on top. Set the slow cooker to LOW and go to sleep. It will be ready in 8 hours. Alternatively, you can pour the mixture into a Dutch oven and bake for 8 hours at 200°F (93°F).

Goes great with a mixed greens salad tossed with lemon vinaigrette.

Butter and nonstick spray, for slow cooker

5 breakfast sausage links, sliced

8 large eggs

2 cups (475 ml) milk

1 cup (30 g) chopped spinach

1 cup (150 g) goat cheese crumbles

¼ cup (30 g) shredded cheddar cheese

1 tbsp (18 g) salt

1 tsp freshly ground black pepper

½ cup (50 g) shredded Parmesan cheese

Lamb Shank
with Orange Gremolata

I never really appreciated lamb and actually can't say I remember having it while growing up. The appreciation came when I was working in a Greek restaurant because that is where I had it all the time. This recipe is so simple and I love to serve it with either rice pilaf or garlic herbed mashed potatoes.

Serves 4

Prepare the lamb shank: Season each shank with 1 tablespoon (18 g) of the salt and 1½ teaspoons (3 g) of the black pepper.

Heat a Dutch oven over medium-high heat. Add 1 tablespoon (15 ml) of the grapeseed oil. Add 2 of the shanks to the pot and sear on all sides for 5 to 6 minutes, or until golden brown. Remove from the pot and place on a rack. Add an additional tablespoon (15 ml) of the grapeseed oil to the pot and sear the remaining 2 shanks on all sides in the same manner. Remove from the pot and place with the other 2 shanks. Add the last tablespoon (15 ml) of grapeseed oil to the pot.

Add the carrots, celery, onion and garlic to the pot and sauté until lightly browned, about 8 minutes. Add the wine and beef base. Make sure you scrape the bottom of the pot to get up all the yumminess. Add the cloves and peppercorns. Return the shanks to the pot and bring to a boil. Lower the heat to medium-low and cover. Cook the shanks over low heat for 8 hours 30 minutes, or until fork-tender. Remove the shanks and set aside on a plate to cool for 25 minutes. Meanwhile, bring the broth to a boil and reduce by one-quarter, then remove from the heat and set aside.

Prepare the gremolata: In a small bowl, combine all the gremolata ingredients, including the olive oil (if using). This can be made while the shanks are cooking. Serve on the side.

Lamb Shank

4 lamb shanks

¼ cup (72 g) salt, divided

2 tbsp (12 g) freshly ground black pepper, divided

3 tbsp (45 ml) grapeseed oil, divided

2 carrots, peeled and diced

2 celery ribs, diced

1 large yellow onion, diced

1 clove garlic, smashed

2 cups (475 ml) red wine

2 cups (475 ml) beef or vegetable base

2 whole cloves

1 tbsp (5 g) whole black peppercorns

Orange Gremolata

Zest of 1 orange

3 tbsp (12 g) chopped fresh parsley

1 clove garlic, minced

1 tbsp (15 ml) olive oil (optional)

Salt and freshly ground black pepper

Duck Confit
with Apple & Celeriac Salad

Duck confit is a traditional French dish that uses the legs of a duck. They are salted, seasoned with fresh herbs and slowly cooked in their own fat. To preserve the confit, you will cool and store it in its own fat. This is a really easy recipe that can even use chicken legs instead of duck. There are two parts to this recipe and I promise the end result will be worth it.

Serves 4

Duck Confit

5 tbsp (94 g) kosher salt

2 cloves garlic, chopped

1 orange rind

5 tbsp (28 g) juniper berries, crushed

3 sprigs thyme

2 bay leaves

4 duck legs or thighs

4 cups (946 ml) melted duck fat (see Notes, next page)

You will need to cure your duck for at least 48 hours. In a bowl, mix together the salt, garlic, orange rind, juniper berries, thyme and bay leaves. Place the duck legs in a casserole dish, making sure they are not overlapping. Spread the salt mixture over the duck legs and make sure you evenly distribute the mixture. Cover and refrigerate for 48 hours.

Remove from the refrigerator and brush off the excess seasonings. Pat the duck legs dry. Preheat your oven to 225°F (110°C). Place the duck legs, skin side down, in a Dutch oven. Pour in the melted duck fat and make sure the duck legs are submerged in the fat. Top with the lid and place in the oven to cook for 4 hours.

At the 4-hour mark, remove from the oven and see whether the meat can pull away from the bone. If the meat pulls away, the legs are done. If the meat is still a bit tough, place back in the oven for another hour.

Apple & Celeriac Salad

2 large Granny Smith apples

1 celeriac

Juice of 2 lemons

¼ cup (60 ml) cider vinegar

1 tsp whole-grain mustard

½ cup (120 ml) olive oil

Salt and freshly ground black pepper

¼ cup (15 g) finely chopped curly parsley

½ cup (30 g) celery leaves

½ cup (50 g) walnuts, crushed (optional)

Prepare the salad: Core the apples and peel the celeriac, then julienne them, making sure you drizzle them with the lemon juice to prevent browning.

In a small bowl, whisk together the cider vinegar and mustard. Slowly, while still whisking, incorporate the olive oil. Continue to whisk to emulsify the dressing. Season with salt and pepper.

In a large bowl, combine the apple, celeriac, parsley, celery leaves and walnuts (if using). Add the dressing and mix well.

· ·

Notes: To preserve the meat, simply keep the chilled duck submerged in the duck fat and store in the refrigerator.

You can replace the duck fat with pork fat, or if you cannot find either, submerge in oil.

*See photo on page 28.

Pork Belly Tacos

Pork belly, by far, is one of those things that I cannot get enough of. Now, when you have tacos-meet-pork belly, you are secretly having a party in your mouth. This recipe is definitely an explosion of flavors. These are sweet, spicy, salty and bitter, making them the BOMB.

Serves 4

Place the pork belly in a casserole dish. In a small bowl, mix together the sugar, salt and black pepper, then evenly distribute and rub onto the pork belly. Cover with plastic wrap and refrigerate for 12 to 15 hours.

Remove from the fridge, unwrap and pat the moisture from the pork belly. Preheat your oven to 450°F (230°C).

In a small bowl, combine the cayenne, smoked paprika and dark chili powder. Rub the pork belly with this mixture and place, fat side up, in a Dutch oven. Place in the oven and roast the pork for 30 minutes. At the 15-minute mark, mix the pineapple with the oil and place on a rimmed cookie sheet. Roast in the oven for 15 minutes. Remove from the oven and set aside.

Lower the oven temperature to 225°F (110°C). Roast the pork belly for an additional 1 hour 45 minutes, or until fork-tender.

Remove from the oven and let the pork cool completely, at least 1 hour. Slice into ¼- to ½-inch (6- to 13-mm) slices and set aside.

In a small bowl, combine the Cilantro-Lime Crema with the sriracha. Mix well and set aside.

Reheat the sliced pork belly in a sauté pan over medium heat until golden brown on both sides, 3 to 4 minutes per side.

To serve, heat the tortillas and place several pieces of pork belly on each tortilla. Add some shredded cabbage, drizzle with the crema mixture and top with the pineapple and Cotija cheese. Garnish with the cilantro and lime wedges.

3 lb (1.4 kg) skinless pork belly

3 tbsp (39 g) sugar

3 tbsp (56 g) kosher salt

1 tsp freshly ground black pepper

½ tsp cayenne pepper

1 tsp smoked paprika

½ tsp dark chili powder

¼ pineapple, peeled, cored and small diced

1 tbsp (15 ml) olive oil

½ cup (120 ml) Cilantro-Lime Crema (page 129)

1 tbsp (15 ml) sriracha

8 to 10 corn or flour tortillas

1 (8- to 10-oz [225- to 280-g]) bag finely shredded cabbage

¼ cup (25 g) Cotija cheese

Chopped fresh cilantro, for garnish

1 lime, cut into wedges, for garnish

My Favorite Things
to Eat in a Bowl

I love these kinds of meals where you can put everything in one bowl and sit on the couch under a cozy blanket while watching a movie (a scary movie, if you're me). The recipes in this chapter have depth of flavor from the extended cooking time. After all, the flavors have to be right on if they're going to be mixed together in one bowl and still stand out. Have fun with the recipes and make them your own.

Beefed Up Bourguignon

In my culinary school days, we learned this recipe—a traditional French dish of braised beef in red wine. I thought, *why does this recipe sit with me?* I then recalled that the great Julia Child made this recipe on her morning cooking show. I remember her saying, "I enjoy cooking with wine; sometimes I even put it in the food."

Serves 6

Preheat your oven to 225°F (110°C). Heat a Dutch oven over medium to high heat. Wait 5 minutes, then add 1 tablespoon (15 ml) of the olive oil. Add your sliced onion and carrots and get a nice caramelization on them, 5 minutes at the most. Remove them from the pot and set aside.

Add the remaining tablespoon (15 ml) of olive oil and your pearl onions and caramelize those for 5 minutes. Remove the onions from the pot and set aside. Time to add the bacon! Sauté for 1 minute, then add the mushrooms and garlic and sauté for 5 minutes. Remove from the pot and set aside. Add your butter and melt completely until it's nearly at the brown-butter stage.

Season your meat with the salt and pepper, then add to the pot and brown on all sides, 4 to 5 minutes per side. Sprinkle the flour over the beef, stirring, making sure the meat is evenly coated. When you start to smell peanuts coming from the pot, your roux is done. Add your wine and deglaze the pot, making sure you are scraping the bottom to get the good stuff. Add the stock, bay leaves, tomato paste, potatoes, thyme and everything that was set aside. Bring to a boil. Cover, put in the oven and cook for 6 hours (alternatively, transfer at this point to a slow cooker; see Note for cook time and setting). At the 6-hour point, remove from the oven, then remove the lid and test a small piece of beef to make sure it is fork-tender. If it is not, put it back in the oven for up to 30 more minutes. Remove the bay leaves.

This can be served on a plate, in a bowl or eaten directly out of the Dutch oven. I love to eat this with grilled bread or over noodles.

2 tbsp (30 ml) olive oil, divided

1 white onion, sliced

2 carrots, peeled and diced

15 pearl onions

4 slices bacon, cut into strips

4 oz (115 g) button mushrooms, quartered

2 cloves garlic, smashed

3 tbsp (42 g) unsalted butter

3 lb (1.4 kg) stew beef or beef roast, cut into 2" (5-cm) cubes

3 tbsp (54 g) salt

1 tbsp (6 g) freshly ground black pepper

3 tbsp (23 g) all-purpose flour

3 cups (710 ml) red wine

3 cups (710 ml) beef stock (homemade [page 134] or store-bought)

2 bay leaves

1 tbsp (16 g) tomato paste

10 baby potatoes

1 tsp fresh thyme

Note: If using a slow cooker, once you bring everything to a boil on the stovetop, transfer to a slow cooker and cook on the LOW setting for 8 hours.

Piggy Mac

This is the number one menu item at my restaurant. The pork has so many layers of spice and flavor, while the creamy, cheesy mac and cheese is topped with crispy onions. How can you not fall in love with this dish?

Serves 10

Preheat your oven to 325°F (165°C). Place your pork in a casserole dish large enough to fit it. In a bowl, combine the cinnamon, garlic powder, cayenne, onion powder, smoked paprika, brown sugar, kosher salt and black pepper and mix together well. Rub the mixture all over the pork inside and out. Add the cola and rice vinegar to the casserole dish. Cover with aluminum foil and set in the center of the oven. Cook for 4 hours. It is done when you can pull it apart with your fork. Pull all the meat apart and let it sit in the pan juices. Cover and place in the oven on the OFF setting until needed.

Fill a large pot halfway with water. Add the tablespoon (18 g) of salt and bring to a boil. As the water heats, in a bowl, combine the onion and buttermilk. Give it a stir and place in the refrigerator until needed.

On a plate, combine the flour with some salt and black pepper and set aside. Add your pasta to the boiling water and cook over high heat for 5 minutes. Drain the pasta and drizzle with a little bit of vegetable oil to prevent sticking. Spread out evenly on a tray. Place in the refrigerator until needed.

Add the canola oil to a small sauté pan and heat for 6 minutes over medium-high heat. Drain the onion of its buttermilk. Dredge the onion in the flour, shake off any excess and, making sure to work in batches, deep-fry for 4 minutes, turning halfway through. When golden brown, remove from the oil and transfer to a plate lined with several layers of paper towels. Set aside until needed.

In a large pot, heat your cream over medium heat. Bring to a simmer and add your cheeses and the pasta. Simmer for 4 minutes, constantly stirring to avoid sticking.

To plate, spread half of the pulled pork evenly in a square dish at least 2 inches (5 cm) deep. Drizzle your favorite barbecue sauce over the meat. Spread the macaroni and cheese evenly on top of the pork so you cannot see the pork. Add the rest of the pork, but this time, place it in the middle of the mac and cheese. Drizzle with barbecue sauce and top with the crispy onions. Time to eat.

1 (4- to 6-lb [1.8- to 2.7-kg]) boneless pork shoulder or pork butt

1 tsp ground cinnamon

1 tbsp (9 g) garlic powder

1 tsp cayenne pepper

1 tsp onion powder

1 tbsp (7 g) smoked paprika

1 tsp light brown sugar

1 tbsp (18 g) kosher salt

1 tsp freshly ground black pepper

½ cup (120 ml) cola

¼ cup (60 ml) rice vinegar

1 tbsp (18 g) salt, to cook pasta

1 white onion, peeled and cut in paper-thin rounds

½ cup (120 ml) buttermilk

2½ cups (313 g) all-purpose flour

Freshly ground black pepper

1 lb (455 g) dried elbow pasta

Vegetable oil, for pasta

1 cup (240 ml) canola oil

2 qt (1.9 L) heavy cream

1 cup (115 g) shredded cheddar cheese

½ cup (60 g) shredded Gruyère cheese

¼ cup (29 g) shredded provolone

Your favorite barbecue sauce

Lamb & Squash Soup

Way early in my culinary career, I worked for a Moroccan chef who was really hard on all of us. Once a week, we ran this amazing soup special and the chef would not give us the recipe. I had to find out what was in it. I broke down every ingredient, every flavor, and figured it out. The flavors are bold and layered. The touch of cinnamon and coriander gives this dish an extra level of depth. With a little bit of this and a little bit of that, this soup will have you coming back for more!

Serves 4

Heat a Dutch oven over medium-high heat. Add your olive oil and heavily season your lamb shank with salt and pepper. Sear the shank on all sides, until golden brown, about 4 minutes per side. Remove the shank, setting it aside on a plate, and add your bacon to the pot. Cook the bacon until golden brown and remove with a slotted spoon. Transfer to a paper towel–lined plate to drain. Remove only some of the bacon grease from the pot, leaving around 2 tablespoons (30 ml) in the pot. Add your onion and sauté over medium heat until caramelized, 5 to 7 minutes. Add your garlic and make sure to move it around so it doesn't burn. Add your bell pepper, carrot and celery at this time. Cook, stirring, for 5 minutes. Add your tomato paste and deglaze the pot with ¾ cup (175 ml) of the chicken stock, making sure you are scraping the bottom.

Add the remaining 5¼ cups (1.3 L) of stock as well as the pinto beans, butternut squash, kale and the lamb shank.

Add your bay leaves, ground cinnamon and coriander and bring to a boil. Lower the heat to low, cover and cook for 6 hours, or until the lamb shank is tender enough for you to shred the meat off it.

Once the shank is tender, remove from the soup. Remove the meat from the bone and give it a rough chop. Return the meat to the soup and cook, uncovered, for another 30 minutes. Remove the bay leaves.

Garnish with the raisins, bacon and parsley.

1 tbsp (15 ml) olive oil

1 small lamb shank

Salt and freshly ground black pepper

3 slices bacon, cut into strips

½ onion, diced

2 cloves garlic, smashed

1 red bell pepper, seeded and diced

1 carrot, peeled and small diced

1 rib celery, small diced

1 tsp tomato paste

6 cups (1.4 L) chicken stock (homemade [page 136] or store-bought), divided

½ cup (100 g) dried pinto beans, soaked overnight in water, drained and rinsed

1 small butternut squash, peeled, seeded and cut into 1" (2.5-cm) chunks

2 cups (134 g) chopped kale

2 bay leaves

½ tsp ground cinnamon

1 tsp ground coriander

¼ cup (35 g) raisins, for garnish

¼ cup (15 g) chopped fresh flat-leaf parsley, for garnish

Smoked Corn Chowder

One day, I thought, I love how my Smoked & Grilled Corn Relish (page 119) is fresh, vibrant and smoky; I wonder whether I can get that effect with a soup. I tried several times and finally figured out the best way to achieve the smokiness. This recipe has some steps to it, but you will enjoy it!

Serves 4 to 6

Pull back the husk on each corn ear. Remove the silk but do not remove the husk. Fold the husk back up and soak the ears of the corn in cold water for 1 hour 30 minutes. While the corn is soaking, separately soak your wood chips in water for 45 minutes.

Heat your grill to 275°F (140°C). Once it is at temperature, shut off one side of your grill. Use aluminum foil to make a pocket by folding the foil in half and then folding each side inward. Drain your chips, place inside the pocket and close the pocket by folding the flap. Poke several holes in the top and bottom of the pocket and place on the hottest side of the grill. When the wood chips start to smoke, move them over to the cold side of the grill.

Place your soaked corn ears on the cold side of the grill and smoke for 1 hour 30 minutes. Remove your corn from the smoker and remove the husk. Use a sharp knife to cut the kernels off each ear, placing them in a bowl. Toss with the thyme. In a stockpot, combine the corn cobs with the cream and half of your corn kernels. Cook, uncovered, over medium-low heat for 2 hours, making sure to stir every 30 minutes or so to prevent a film from forming. You want to reduce the mixture by half. Remove from the heat and discard the cobs. When the mixture has cooled for 10 minutes, transfer it to a blender. Do this in batches so the steam doesn't make the blender overflow. Add your butter in batches while blending. Line a fine-mesh strainer or a colander with several layers of cheesecloth and pour the mixture through it and back into its pot. Make sure, if using cheesecloth, that you push through any extra liquid with a wooden spoon.

In a saucepan, combine your diced potatoes with enough water to cover and bring to a boil. Cook, uncovered, for 15 minutes. Drain the potatoes. Add the remaining corn kernels and potatoes to the corn stock. Season with salt and pepper to taste and garnish with the bacon crumbles.

4 ears corn in husk

1 cup (90 g) apple wood chips

2 tsp (2 g) fresh thyme

1 gal (3.8 L) heavy cream

1 lb (455 g) unsalted butter, cubed

8 oz (225 g) yellow potatoes, peeled and cut into ¼" (6-mm) cubes

Salt and freshly ground black pepper

½ cup (60 g) bacon crumbles, for garnish

Healthy, Hearty Spinach, Sausage & Bean Soup

This is a healthy yet filling soup that is layered with bold flavors. It is great for lunch or a hearty dinner with a grilled cheese sandwich on the side. I like to make extra so I can have leftovers. When portioned correctly, this soup is easy to freeze. I like to use leftover Chinese soup containers, or if you have vacuum-seal bags, you can seal the soup in quart (liter)-size bags and freeze.

Serves 4 to 6

Preheat your oven to 200°F (90°C).

Heat a Dutch oven over medium-high heat. Add the oil and your sausages. Season with salt and the dried sage. Cook on all sides, stirring often, about 2 minutes per side, or until lightly browned. Remove the sausage and set aside in a bowl. Add the celery, carrot, onion and garlic to the pot and cook for 3 minutes.

Add your chicken stock and scrape the bottom of the pot with a wooden spoon. Add the beans, bay leaves and sausage. Bring to a boil and cover. Place in the oven and cook for 7 hours.

Remove from the oven and add the spinach and thyme. Stir until the spinach is wilted. Remove the bay leaves before serving.

Note: To speed up the cooking process, preheat the oven to 300°F (150°C) and cook for 3 hours 30 minutes. The flavors will be bold but not as bold as if you cooked it for the time noted above.

1 tbsp (15 ml) vegetable oil

2 links apple chicken sausages, cooked and cut into ¼" (6-mm) pieces

2 maple-flavored sausages, cooked and cut into ¼" (6-mm) pieces

2 andouille sausages, cut into thin rounds

Salt

1 tsp dried sage

2 ribs celery, small diced

1 large carrot, peeled, small diced

1 white onion, small diced

3 cloves garlic, smashed

5 cups (1.2 L) chicken stock (homemade [page 136] or store-bought)

2 (15-oz [425-g]) cans northern beans, drained and rinsed

3 bay leaves

3 cups (90 g) baby spinach

1 tbsp (3 g) fresh thyme, minced

All about That Bisque

Lobster bisque is by far one of my favorite soups to make and eat. This recipe is perfect for those nights that you are at work late and know that you won't have enough time to cook dinner. This can be prepped the night before and then, when you wake up, remove the slow cooker from the fridge and let it cook all day. By the time you get home, the soup will be finished and all you need to do is add the finishing touches.

Serves 4 to 6

Heat a sauté pan over medium to high heat. Add the oil to the pan. Sauté the lobster tails until they turn red, about 3 minutes. Remove the tails from the pan and set aside while you proceed through the next step.

Add the shallots, garlic and celery and sauté until translucent, 3 to 4 minutes. Deglaze the pan with the brandy and cognac. Cook until the mixture reduces by half. Add your seafood stock, tomato paste, Creole seasoning, white pepper and cream. Cook, stirring, for 5 minutes, then pour into a 6- to 8-quart (5.7- to 7.6-L) slow cooker.

Remove the lobster meat from the shells and dice into small pieces. Place in the refrigerator until later.

Set the slow cooker to LOW and cook for 7 hours. At the 7-hour point, puree the soup in batches in a blender, dividing the butter among the batches.

Add the thyme and place back in the slow cooker. At this time, you will add the diced lobster. Cook for 5 minutes on high and then the soup will be ready.

This goes great with crackers or a grilled cheese sandwich.

1 tbsp (15 ml) oil

4 lobster tails

2 shallots, minced

1 clove garlic, minced

¼ cup (30 g) small-diced celery

2 tbsp (30 ml) brandy

2 tbsp (30 ml) cognac

4 cups (946 ml) seafood stock

1 tbsp (16 g) tomato paste

½ tsp Creole seasoning

½ tsp ground white pepper

1 cup (240 ml) heavy cream

2 tbsp (28 g) unsalted butter

1 tsp fresh thyme

Party *Favorites*

No matter whether you're having a small get-together or a huge Sunday football party, these recipes will make any gathering a hit.

The recipes in this chapter consist of the heavy hitters, the ones that really stand out and make a difference—like wings, ribs and sliders. One of my favorites among them is my wings (page 89), whose sticky sweetness will have you begging for game day.

Game Day Wings

I own a kitchen at a local bar and we are known for our wings. You can't be a great bar with yucky wings. You will fall in love with this recipe. The meat just falls off the bone. Then toss them in our famous wing sauce on page 125. These wings are sure to be the hit at any party.

Serves 4

Preheat your oven to 275°F (140°C). Line a baking sheet with aluminum foil.

Meanwhile, place the wings in a large bowl and add ½ cup (120 ml) of the oil. In a separate bowl, mix together the paprika, granulated garlic, onion powder, cayenne, salt and black pepper. When that mixture is fully incorporated, use it to season the wings.

Arrange the seasoned wings in a single layer on the prepared baking sheet. Place in the oven and let them cook for 2 hours.

At the 2-hour point, heat vegetable oil in your deep fryer. If you do not have a deep fryer, you can fill a large saucepan halfway with oil; you will have to cook the wings in more batches this way.

When the wings are done, remove from the oven and let cool for 10 minutes before putting in the fryer. If you like a flour crust, you may dredge them in rice flour, making sure to shake off any excess flour. Working in batches so as not to overcrowd the pot, submerge the wings (dredged or not) in the oil for 7 to 8 minutes, or until they reach your desired texture.

Transfer the fried wings to a rack set over a paper towel–lined sheet pan so the excess oil may drain, and season them with salt and pepper.

Grab your wing sauce and toss your wings. Serve with ranch or blue cheese dressing.

3 lb (1.4 kg) chicken wings

½ cup (120 ml) vegetable oil, plus more for frying

8 tbsp (55 g) paprika

6 tbsp (54 g) granulated garlic

¼ cup (28 g) onion powder

1 tsp cayenne pepper

3 tbsp (54 g) salt, plus more to taste

4 tbsp (28 g) freshly ground black pepper, plus more to taste

Rice flour (optional)

My Famous Wing Sauce (page 125)

Ranch or blue cheese dressing, for serving

The Best Meat Sliders Around

These are the best little things ever! Meat and cheese as a sauce—how can you go wrong? I would sell out of these little guys at every food truck event I attended. No matter how many balls I rolled, it still wasn't enough.

Serves 10

Preheat your oven to 225°F (110°C). Heat a Dutch oven over medium to high heat. Meanwhile, you can start to make your meatballs if their mixture was not prepared ahead of time.

Place the ground chuck in a large bowl. Add the eggs, Parmesan cheese, red pepper flakes, dried basil, granulated garlic, balsamic vinegar, bread crumbs, fresh basil, salt and cold water. Gently mix until everything is incorporated. Roll into 2-inch (5-cm) balls and set aside on a plate.

When the Dutch oven is heated, add the oil and, working in batches so as not to overcrowd the pot, sear the meatballs on all sides, 2 minutes per side, transferring them to a plate as each batch is seared. When finished searing all the meatballs, put all of them back in the pot. Add your tomato sauce and salt and pepper to taste, cover and cook in the oven for 3 hours.

At the 3-hour mark, layer your mozzarella and provolone cheese over the meatballs. Set your broiler to HIGH and place the Dutch oven in the middle of the oven. Let the cheese get all melty and golden for 5 minutes. Remove from the oven and sprinkle with Parmesan cheese and chiffonaded fresh basil.

To serve, scoop out a ball and place it inside a dinner roll.

Note: The meatball mixture can be made in advance and stored in the fridge for up to 24 hours.

1½ lb (680 g) ground chuck

2 large eggs, beaten

½ cup (50 g) grated Parmesan cheese, plus more for garnish

1 tbsp (4 g) red pepper flakes

1 tbsp (2 g) dried basil

1 tbsp (9 g) granulated garlic

1 tsp balsamic vinegar

1 cup (115 g) bread crumbs

3 leaves fresh basil, chiffonaded (see Note, page 14), plus more for garnish

1½ tsp (9 g) salt, plus more to taste

1 cup (240 ml) cold water

1 tbsp (15 ml) vegetable oil

2 (8-oz [225-g]) cans tomato sauce

Freshly ground black pepper

10 slices fresh mozzarella cheese

6 slices provolone cheese

Crunchy dinner rolls (try frozen parcooked French rolls if you cannot find in a bakery)

Short Rib Chili *with Cornbread*

What better thing to have on a cold day than a bowl of chili with some cornbread? I don't like ground beef chili because of the texture, so in this recipe we're going to use short rib. You can also use flap steak instead of short ribs, which is a good substitute if your market does not have any short ribs.

With this recipe, you are building layers and layers of flavor. The longer it cooks and sits, the better result you get.

Serves 6 to 8

2 lb (906 g) boneless short ribs or flap steak

Salt and freshly ground black pepper

1 tbsp (15 ml) olive oil

½ white onion, small diced

1 jalapeño pepper, minced, with seeds

1 red bell pepper, seeded and small diced

8 oz (240 ml) Guinness

2 (16-oz [455-g]) cans crushed tomatoes

1 cup (240 ml) beef stock (homemade [page 134] or store-bought)

1 tbsp (16 g) tomato paste

3 bay leaves

8 oz (225 g) small dried red beans

½ tsp ground cinnamon

2 tbsp (15 g) dark chili powder

1 tbsp (8 g) light chili powder

1 tbsp (7 g) onion powder

1 tbsp (9 g) granulated garlic

1 tsp cayenne pepper

2 cups (475 ml) boiling water

2 dried guajillo chiles

2 dried ancho chiles

1 tsp unsweetened cocoa powder

1 tbsp (3 g) dried oregano

½ bunch cilantro, minced, plus more for garnish

½ (8-oz [225-g]) can chipotle peppers in adobo sauce, blended

1 tsp ground cumin

1 cup (28 g) crushed tortilla chips, divided

Classic Crema (page 126), for garnish

Juice of 2 limes

(Continued)

Short Rib Chili *with Cornbread*
continued

We are going to use a Dutch oven and a 6- to 8-quart (5.7- to 7.6-L) slow cooker for this recipe.

Heat your Dutch oven over medium-high heat. While it heats, season your short ribs heavily with salt and black pepper on all sides. Add the olive oil and sear the short ribs on all sides for 3 to 4 minutes per side. Remove the short ribs from the pot and add your onion, jalapeño and bell pepper. Sauté until the onion is translucent and the peppers have a nice caramelization, about 3 minutes.

Deglaze the pot with the Guinness, making sure to use a spatula to get all the yumminess on the bottom. Add the crushed tomatoes, beef stock and tomato paste. Give it a nice stir. Return the short ribs to the pot and add all the remaining ingredients, except the crushed tortilla chips, crema and lime juice, reserving some of the cilantro for garnish.

Bring to a boil. Add half of the crushed tortillas and make sure they are incorporated. Pour the mixture into the slow cooker and set on low. Forget about it for 8 hours. That's correct, 8 hours. Uncover and stir in the rest of the crushed tortilla chips. Garnish with minced cilantro, a drizzle of crema and lime juice. Serve with my Kickin' Cornbread (page 111).

Sticky Drumsticks
with Watermelon Salad

I love, love, love drumsticks! This is a great barbecue recipe for a day out in the park. The sweet, salty, Asian flavors that the drumsticks are marinated in goes great with the fresh watermelon salad. The freshness of the salad cuts through any heaviness from the drummies. This is a recipe that your friends will ask you for again and again.

Serves 4 to 6

Prepare the drumsticks: In a bowl, whisk together the honey, balsamic vinegar, soy sauce, garlic, ginger and shallots until fully incorporated. Divide the mixture between 2 gallon-size (3.8-L) ziplock freezer bags and add 6 drumsticks to each bag. Seal the bags and put in the refrigerator to marinate for 4 hours.

When ready to cook, preheat your oven to 200°F (90°C) and line a baking sheet with aluminum foil.

Meanwhile, heat a Dutch oven over medium heat. Remove the drumsticks from their marinade, reserving the marinade, and pat dry. Heat the oil in a Dutch oven over medium heat.

Working in batches, sear the drumsticks on all sides for 3 to 4 minutes per side, making sure you continuously move the legs; you don't want the chicken to burn due to the marinade. Set the cooked drumsticks aside on a plate until all are seared.

Place the drumsticks on the prepared baking sheet and place in the oven on the middle rack. In a saucepan, bring the leftover marinade to a quick boil. Lower the heat to medium and let the marinade reduce for 15 minutes to thicken. Bake the drumsticks for 4 hours, basting every hour with the reduced marinade, making sure you rotate to evenly coat the legs.

(Continued)

Drumsticks

¼ cup (85 g) honey

½ cup (120 ml) balsamic vinegar

½ cup (120 ml) low-sodium soy sauce

2 cloves garlic, minced

1 tsp ground ginger

2 shallots, minced

12 chicken drumsticks

1 tbsp (15 ml) olive oil

¼ cup (10 g) chopped cilantro, for garnish

Sticky Drumsticks *with Watermelon Salad* *continued*

At the 4-hour mark, turn on your broiler and baste the drumsticks again. Rotate under the broiler for 3 to 5 minutes. Make sure they don't burn. You're looking for the marinade to stick to the legs. When the drumsticks are finished, remove from the oven, transfer to a platter and sprinkle with the cilantro.

Prepare the salad: In a bowl, gently combine the watermelon, onion and goat cheese. Season with the salt, then toss with the arugula. Sprinkle with the sunflower seeds and drizzle the top with the balsamic glaze; it's your decision how much you want to drizzle.

Watermelon Salad

1 small seedless watermelon, cut into ½" (1.3-cm) cubes

1 red onion, peeled and shaved

½ cup (75 g) crumbled goat cheese

1 tsp salt

2 cups (40 g) baby arugula

½ cup (72 g) toasted sunflower seeds

Balsamic glaze, for garnish

2-Steppin' Spare Ribs

Rubs and ribs. Mmmmmmm. Need I say more? Doing a dry rub intensifies the flavor while the cola on the bottom gives a nice braising liquid with a touch of sweetness. This is great when paired with a light salad.

Serves 2 to 4

On the back of the rib rack is a thin layer of skin known as silver skin, which needs to be removed. To do so, dry off the ribs with a paper towel. Starting at the corner of the ribs by the top bone, use a piece of paper towel to grip the skin tightly, then use the paper towel to peel the skin off the bone. If you have a hard time peeling it off this way, use a butter knife to remove it.

In a bowl, whisk together the brown sugar, granulated garlic, onion powder, smoked paprika, dry mustard, cayenne, salt and black pepper. Sprinkle the front and back of the ribs, making sure you coat the rack evenly and generously. Instead of rubbing in the mixture, pat it on.

Cover and put the ribs in the fridge to let the flavors settle in and marinate for at least 24 hours.

The next day, preheat the oven to 250°F (120°C). Put the ribs on a baking rack placed inside a deep baking pan big enough to hold the rack. Add the cola and cider vinegar to the bottom of the pan. Cook at 250°F (120°C) for 5 hours, basting the ribs every hour. At the end of the last hour, fire up a grill—I like to use a charcoal grill for this. To test whether the ribs are tender, give one of the bones a little shake. If it moves, it is ready. If not, bake for 30 more minutes, or until the bones can be moved.

Remove the rib rack from the pan, transferring the pan juices to a saucepan. Add the ketchup, molasses and hot sauce to the juices and bring to a boil. Cook for 3 to 5 minutes, then remove from the heat and set aside.

Once the ribs are ready, put them on the grill to get nice marks for about 6 minutes per side, starting meat side down and then flipping them over, basting the ribs on both sides with the homemade barbecue sauce.

1 (3- to 4-lb [1.4- to 1.8-kg]) rack spare ribs

1 tbsp (15 g) light brown sugar

1 tbsp (9 g) granulated garlic

1½ tsp (4 g) onion powder

1½ tsp (4 g) smoked paprika

1½ tsp (5 g) dry mustard

1½ tsp (3 g) cayenne pepper

1 tbsp (18 g) salt

1 tbsp (6 g) freshly ground black pepper

2 cups (475 ml) cola

½ cup (120 ml) cider vinegar

¼ cup (55 ml) ketchup

1½ tsp (8 g) molasses

2 dashes of hot sauce

Slow-Roasted Pork Sandwich

I love to make this recipe on game days. It calls for the leftovers from the Slow-Roasted Pork Butt (page 55). I usually make the pork recipe on a Saturday, which works out well for our Sunday Fundays, when there are anywhere from six to ten of us having a great time hanging out and playing games. Everyone brings something to the table and this is one of my go-to recipes. The sweetness and spiciness of the pork complements the saltiness of the crispy fried onions and the hints of pepper from the arugula. It's a game changer.

Serves 4 (2 sliders each)

In a sauté pan, heat 1 tablespoon (15 ml) of the olive oil and add the pork and yellow onion. Cook until the onion caramelizes, about 7 minutes, then season with half of the paprika, half of the garlic powder and half of the salt.

In a medium-size saucepan, heat the remaining tablespoon (15 ml) of olive oil over medium heat for 5 minutes. Drain the red onion from the buttermilk. In a bowl, mix together the flour and remaining paprika, garlic, salt and drained red onion. When the olive oil is hot, shake any excess flour from the onion and fry in small batches until golden brown, about 4 minutes. Remove the fried red onion from the oil and place on a rack set over a pan to drain. Finish draining on a paper towel–lined pan to absorb any additional grease.

In a small sauté pan over medium heat, heat 2 tablespoons (30 ml) of the canola oil and sauté the julienned yellow onion, stirring continuously, until caramelized, 7 to 8 minutes.

In a small bowl, mix together the mayonnaise, lemon juice and zest and set aside.

Open your buns and apply the mayonnaise mixture to the inner top and bottom. Place the arugula in a bowl and drizzle olive oil around the inner side of the bowl. Season with salt and pepper. Gently fold the arugula around the bowl to incorporate the oil. Place a little bit of arugula on the bottom of the buns. Add your pork mixture and then top with the crispy red onion and caramelized yellow onion. Add the top bun and make sure you taste test one of the sandwiches.

2 tbsp (30 ml) olive oil, divided, plus more for garnish

10 oz (280 g) leftover pork from Slow-Roasted Pork Butt (page 55), shredded

1 yellow onion, thinly sliced

2 tbsp (14 g) paprika, divided

2 tbsp (18 g) garlic powder, divided

2 tbsp (36 g) salt, divided

1 red onion, sliced paper thin and soaked in buttermilk with 5 dashes of Tabasco sauce for 30 minutes

3 cups (375 g) all-purpose flour

2 tbsp (30 ml) canola oil

1 yellow onion, julienned

1 cup (225 g) mayonnaise

Zest and juice of 1 lemon

8 slider buns

2 cups (40 g) arugula

Salt and freshly ground black pepper

Ropa Vieja Empanadas

We are always eating empanadas at my house when we have ropa from the night before. This recipe uses Ropa Vieja (page 25), but you could use meat from Momma Duke's Chicken Tacos (page 22) instead. This goes great with the homemade Cilantro-Lime Crema (page 129).

Serves 4 to 6

This will be easy if you have an empanada press; you should be able to find one at any local store. If you do not have one, that is fine; we can make it the old-fashioned way.

Take an empanada wrapper and place it on a clean countertop. Then, place about 1 ounce (28 g) of your meat mixture in the center of the wrapper. If you like, this is where you can add cheese. Add some of the eggs and olives to the filling.

Fold the wrapper over to make a half-moon. Make sure you remove any extra air by starting from the center where the meat is and then pushing down on the wrapper to make a smooth seal. This is a 1-step process with an empanada maker; but if you don't have one, fold by hand and use a fork to press the curved edge of the wrapper closed. I then like to roll up the empanada to make it pretty for presentation.

There are 2 ways we can cook this. The first is in a deep fryer or sauté pan filled with oil, cooking on both sides until golden brown, 3 minutes per side. Place the fried empanadas on a paper towel–lined plate to absorb any oil.

The second way is to preheat your oven to 325°F (165°C). Line a cookie sheet with parchment paper and then spray with nonstick spray. Place the empanadas on the prepared pan, making sure they aren't overcrowded (no more than 8 to 10 per pan), then cover them and bake for 12 minutes, or until golden brown.

10 empanada wrappers, such as Goya brand

10 oz (280 g) leftover Ropa Vieja meat (page 25), divided, kept cold

½ cup (58 g) shredded Jack cheese, divided (optional)

3 hard-boiled large eggs, diced

3 olives, diced

Vegetable oil, if frying (optional)

Nonstick spray, if baking (optional)

Great Slow
Side Dishes

You can't have a complete meal without some banging side dishes. These take a bit longer than the traditional side dishes we may be used to, but a lot of the recipes are set and forget. Let them cook slow and low to build the best and deepest flavors.

Dutch Oven Bread

This, by far, is the best-tasting bread recipe. It takes some time, but I promise you the end result will be worth the wait. When you cut into this bread, you will instantly smell how delicious it is going to taste. The crunchy outside with the moist, soft inside will make this one of your favorite and easiest recipes. The key is patience.

Serves 8

In a bowl, combine the warm water and active dry yeast. Give a quick stir and allow the yeast to bloom. You can tell it's ready when it gets foamy.

In a large bowl, mix together 3½ cups (435 g) of the flour and the kosher salt. Make a well in the center and pour in the yeast mixture. Using your hands, gently incorporate the yeast and flour mixtures. Mix until you achieve a doughlike texture that pulls away from the sides of the bowl. If too sticky, add 1 tablespoon (18 g) of flour.

Once the dough comes together, cover the bowl and allow the dough to rise for at least 15 hours and no more than 18 hours. When the dough has risen, use a spatula to scrape down the sides of the bowl to loosen up the dough.

Sprinkle some flour on a clean countertop and turn the dough out of the bowl onto the lightly floured countertop. Lightly punch it down and then form a ball, seam side down. Sprinkle with a teaspoon of flour, cover and let rest for another hour.

Preheat your oven to 450°F (230°C). Place a lidded Dutch oven inside and let it heat up. Using oven mitts, remove the heated pot from the oven and remove the lid. Place the proofed dough inside the pot. Don't worry about shaping the bread; it will expand to fit the pot. Brush the top of the dough with the olive oil and sprinkle with the sea salt to evenly cover the top. Using a paring knife, slightly score the dough twice on top.

Cover the pot and place it back in the oven. Cook, covered, for 30 minutes, then remove the lid and cook for an additional 15 minutes, or until the top is lightly golden brown.

Remove from the pot and let cool before slicing. This goes great with honey butter!

2 cups (475 ml) water, warmed to 90 to 110°F (32 to 43°C)

1 (0.75-oz [21-g]) packet active dry yeast

3½ cups (435 g) all-purpose flour, plus more as needed

½ tsp kosher salt

1 tsp olive oil

1 tsp sea salt

Puerto Rican Red Beans

Growing up, I spent summers at my grandparents' house in Orlando. This side dish was a main component to every dinner that I had there. It goes great with any protein or on top of a bowl of white rice and a sunny-side-up egg. The levels of flavor that you will taste from the final product will make you giddy with excitement.

Serves 8

Drain and rinse the soaked beans.

In a food processor, combine your peppers, garlic, cilantro and onion. Pulse until the mixture is almost smooth; you still want some texture. Add 1 tablespoon (15 ml) of the vegetable oil. Pulse again.

Heat a large saucepan over medium heat and add the remaining tablespoon (15 ml) of oil. Transfer the pepper mixture from the processor to the pot. Add your tomato paste and stir for 1 minute. Now, add your vegetable broth and olive brine. Add the beans and potatoes, then the culantro, Sazón, granulated garlic, onion powder, hot sauce and olives and bring to a quick boil. Cover, lower the heat to low and cook for 1 hour 15 minutes. The beans should have a nice sauce and the potatoes should be fork-tender.

1½ cups (300 g) dried red beans, soaked overnight in several inches of water

½ green bell pepper, seeded and chopped

½ red bell pepper, seeded and chopped

3 cloves garlic, smashed

½ bunch cilantro, minced

½ white onion, chopped

2 tbsp (30 ml) vegetable oil, divided

2 tbsp (32 g) tomato paste

2 cups (475 ml) vegetable broth (homemade [page 137] or store-bought)

2 tbsp (30 ml) manzanilla olive brine

3 Idaho potatoes, peeled and large diced

2 culantro leaves

2 (0.5-oz [15-g]) packets Sazón

1 tbsp (9 g) granulated garlic

1 tsp onion powder

1½ tsp (8 ml) hot sauce

¼ cup (25 g) manzanilla olives, drained

Kickin' Cornbread

Cornbread is something that can be easily messed up. I've had some really dry ones in my years. I have finally perfected my recipe to make this the moistest cornbread you have ever had.

Serves 12

Spray a 9-inch (23-cm) round cast-iron skillet with nonstick spray and set aside. Preheat your oven to 300°F (150°C).

Sift together the flour, cornmeal, sugar, salt and baking powder into a large bowl. Make a well in the middle of the mixture, add the milk, butter and egg and stir until the mixture has very few lumps.

Pour the batter into the prepared skillet and bake for 1 hour, or until golden brown.

Serve with honey and whipped butter.

Nonstick spray

1 cup (125 g) all-purpose flour

1 cup (140 g) cornmeal

⅔ cup (133 g) sugar

1 tsp salt

3½ tsp (16 g) baking powder

1 cup (240 ml) whole milk

½ cup (120 ml) melted butter

1 large egg

Cuban Black Beans

I came home from work one day and my girlfriend had put together these banging black beans. The aroma that was flowing through the house had me on my tippy toes being drawn to the beans on the stove. Make sure you have leftovers; you're going to want them!

Serves 8

Drain and rinse the soaked beans.

In a Dutch oven over medium heat, heat the oil. Add the bell pepper, onion and garlic. Sauté for 5 minutes, then add the culantro, cilantro and oregano. Add the vinegar and cooking wine and deglaze the bottom of the pot. Add your beans and chicken stock. Add the Sazón, granulated garlic, onion powder and black pepper.

Bring to a boil and make sure you stir. Lower the heat to low, cover and leave for 3 hours. Remove the lid, give a stir and season with salt, if needed.

1½ lb (680 g) dried black beans, soaked overnight in several inches of water

1 tsp olive oil

½ green bell pepper, minced

½ yellow onion, minced

3 cloves garlic, minced

2 culantro leaves, minced

Leaves from 4 sprigs cilantro, minced

Leaves from 1 sprig oregano, minced

1½ tsp (8 ml) red wine vinegar

1 tbsp (15 ml) white cooking wine

2 qt (1.9 L) chicken stock (homemade [page 136] or store-bought)

1 (0.5-oz [15-g]) packet Sazón

1 tsp granulated garlic

1 tsp onion powder

1 tsp freshly ground black pepper

Salt (optional)

Sweet and Spicy Baked Beans

There is no other way to make this—well, there are other ways, but the best way is to use fresh beans. This recipe calls for fresh pinto beans. Baked beans are traditionally made with navy beans, but you can generally use any type of bean. This recipe has smokiness, sweetness and a bit of spice. Adding the sausages gives an added note that makes this dish a popular one in my family's house.

Serves 6

Drain and rinse the soaked beans.

Preheat your oven to 225°F (110°C).

Heat a Dutch oven over medium heat. Add your oil. Render the bacon three-quarters of the way, then remove from the pot and place on a plate. Without draining away the bacon fat, add the onion, jalapeño and serrano pepper to the pot and sauté for 4 minutes. Add your Vienna sausages and return the bacon to the pot. Deglaze the pan with 1 cup (240 ml) of the vegetable broth. Make sure you scrape the yumminess from the bottom. Add the remaining 3 cups (710 ml) of broth, then the molasses, tomato paste, brown sugar, maple syrup, white and black pepper, dry mustard and salt. Bring to a boil. Give a stir, cover and put in the oven to cook for 4 hours.

Remove from the oven. The beans should be tender and the liquid should be sticky. Let sit for 10 to 15 minutes before serving, to thicken up.

1 lb (455 g) dried pinto beans, soaked overnight in several inches of water

1½ tsp (8 ml) canola oil

6 slices bacon, thinly sliced

1 yellow onion, small diced

½ jalapeño pepper, seeded and minced

½ serrano pepper, seeded and minced

3 Vienna sausages, sliced into thin rounds

4 cups (946 ml) vegetable broth (homemade [page 137] or store-bought), divided

1 tbsp (15 g) molasses

1½ tsp (8 g) tomato paste

¼ cup (60 g) light brown sugar

2 tbsp (30 ml) pure maple syrup

1 tsp ground white pepper

1 tsp freshly ground black pepper

1 tsp dry mustard

1½ tsp (9 g) salt

Southern Collard Greens

Collard greens is a staple dish in the South. Living in Georgia for ten years, I have eaten my fair share of collard greens. I decided to take all the different versions I have tried and put everything I love about collards in one simple recipe. The prep in this recipe takes some time, but once it starts cooking, you can set and forget.

Serves 6 to 8

Clean the collard greens in a large pot of cold water. Cut each leaf off its stem and into 1-inch (2.5-cm) pieces. Put the leaves back into the pot and let sit in the cold water for 1 hour. Give a couple of stirs. Take out your collards and drain them in a colander.

Heat a Dutch oven over medium heat and add the oil. Add the bacon; when it is three-quarters of the way rendered, throw in your onions and ham. Cook the onions until translucent, 3 to 4 minutes. Now, add your garlic and red pepper flakes. Sauté for 2 minutes, then add your cider vinegar. Scrape the bottom of the pot to get up any yummies that might have stuck. Add your chicken stock at this point.

Add the collards, pork neck bones and sugar, black pepper, dry mustard, salt, white pepper and hot sauce to the pot. Press the collards down in the liquid and let it come to a simmer. Then, lower the heat to low. Cover and let cook for 4 hours 30 minutes, making sure you stir the collards every hour.

1 lb (455 g) collard greens

1 tsp vegetable oil

12 slices hickory-smoked bacon, small diced

2 yellow onions, small diced

8 oz (225 g) smoked ham, small diced

8 cloves garlic, minced

1 tsp red pepper flakes

2 cups (475 ml) cider vinegar

3½ qt (3.3 L) chicken stock (homemade [page 136] or store-bought)

8 oz (225 g) smoked pork neck bones

2 tbsp (26 g) sugar

½ tsp freshly ground black pepper

1 tsp dry mustard

1 tsp salt

½ tsp ground white pepper

1 tbsp (15 ml) hot sauce

Smoked & Grilled Corn Relish

This is a really easy side dish to make. Smoking the corn first, then grilling it brings out the sweetness and gives it a nice smoky flavor with hints of that necessary bitterness from the grill.

Serves 4 to 6

Pull back the husk on each corn ear. Remove the silk but do not remove the husk. Fold the husk back up and soak the ears of the corn in cold water for at least a couple of hours.

Prepare your barbecue grill or smoker and put your wood chips on the coal. Fold back the corn husks and pat each ear dry. In a bowl, mix together the olive oil, cayenne, paprika and garlic powder. Brush the ears of the corn with the mixture, then fold back the husks and place the corn on the grill. Close the lid and smoke the corn at 220°F (104°C) for 1 hour. Remove the corn and bring the grill to 400°F (200°C). Pull back the husks and grill the corn until grill marks are achieved on all sides.

Remove the corn from the grill and shave off the kernels into a bowl. Add the red onion, bell peppers and jalapeño to the kernels, then the cider vinegar. Stir and season to taste with salt and black pepper. Chill for at least 3 hours before serving.

6 ears corn, in husk

1 cup (90 g) hickory chips, soaked for at least 30 minutes, then drained

¼ cup (60 ml) olive oil

¼ tsp cayenne pepper

¼ tsp paprika

¼ tsp garlic powder

¼ red onion, small diced

½ red bell pepper, seeded and small diced

¼ green bell pepper, seeded and small diced

½ jalapeño pepper, seeded and minced

¼ cup (60 ml) cider vinegar

Salt and freshly ground black pepper

My Momma's Mushrooms

No matter how many times I prepare this recipe, it will never taste like my momma's; that's because it tastes *better*. Sorry, Mom! I prefer using cremini mushrooms instead of button because they have an earthier and meatier texture. These are great as a side at my holiday dinner.

Serves 4

In a medium-sized saucepan, bring the water to a boil. Add the mushrooms and cook, stirring, for 5 minutes. Drain the mushrooms.

Heat a Dutch oven over medium heat. Add the vegetable oil and the drained mushrooms. Let the mushrooms cook for 5 minutes, stirring constantly. Add the minced garlic and red pepper flakes. Lower the heat to low. Add the balsamic vinegar, granulated garlic, salt and onion powder. Stir, then cover and cook for 1 hour 15 minutes, making sure to stir every 20 minutes. If the liquid is reducing to nothing, add up to ¼ cup (60 ml) more water.

4 cups (946 ml) water, plus more if needed

8 oz (225 g) cremini mushrooms

6 tbsp (90 ml) vegetable oil

2 cloves garlic, minced

1 tsp red pepper flakes

2 tbsp (30 ml) balsamic vinegar

1½ tsp (5 g) granulated garlic

1 tsp salt

½ tsp onion powder

It's All about
the Basics

··

In this chapter are the essentials for your kitchen. Stocks, broths and sauces are the best components to keep on hand. The recipes in this chapter are the building blocks that make your dishes complete; they are the bridge to the final product.

My Famous Wing Sauce

I like to consider myself a wings connoisseur. I thought I had had the best buffalo wing sauce in Atlanta, Georgia, at a local restaurant where I used to work . . . until I mastered my own. You will be drinking this sauce—that is how good it is.

Makes 4 cups (946 ml)

Heat a stockpot over medium to high heat. Add the grapeseed oil to the pot and let it get hot to the point right before it smokes; I like to use grapeseed oil because it has a higher smoke point than other oils. Add the onion and sauté almost to caramelization, about 5 minutes. Add the garlic and sauté for 1 minute, then use the red wine vinegar to deglaze the bottom of the pot. Make sure you scrape the bottom of the pot to release the yumminess.

Add everything else, except the xanthan gum. Make sure you whisk all the spices into the sauce mixture. Let the sauce come to a boil, then lower the heat to a simmer and cook for 5 minutes. Lower the heat as low as it can get and cook, covered, for 2 hours, making sure to stir every 15 minutes to prevent sticking. Stir in the xanthan gum at the very end; it is used to help the sauce stick to the wings better.

2 tbsp (30 ml) grapeseed oil

½ yellow onion, diced

2 cloves garlic, minced

½ cup (120 ml) red wine vinegar

2 (12-oz [355-ml]) bottles Crystal Louisiana's Pure Hot Sauce

2 (12-oz [355-ml]) bottles Texas Pete Hot Sauce

12 oz (368 g) tomato sauce

1 cup (240 ml) water

4 tbsp (28 g) paprika

3 tbsp (28 g) granulated garlic

¼ cup (28 g) onion powder

1⅓ cups (28 g) dried parsley

5 tbsp (28 g) cayenne pepper

4 tbsp (28 g) freshly ground black pepper

4½ tsp (28 g) salt

2 tbsp (15 g) xanthan gum

Classic Crema

There is nothing like making your own homemade crema. Sure, you can use regular sour cream, but this tastes better and is more rewarding. I first started making my own crema when I opened the Palate Party food truck. Using the freshest ingredients was the most important thing for my truck. That is what made us stand out. This recipe is one of the easiest things to make. All you have to do is put all the ingredients together and wait for the final result.

Makes 2 cups (475 ml)

In a saucepan, heat the cream over low to medium heat until room temperature. Stir in the buttermilk.

Transfer the mixture to a 1-quart (1-L) Mason jar and place the lid on top. Do not seal. Keep the jar on the counter or in a warm place for 24 hours.

Stir in the lime juice and salt, tighten the lid and refrigerate. You will see in a couple of hours how much it has thickened.

In a few hours, it will thicken even more. Use immediately or keep covered in the refrigerator for up to 2 weeks.

2 cups (475 ml) heavy cream

2 tbsp (30 ml) buttermilk

Juice of 1 lime

Pinch of salt

Cilantro-Lime Crema

A crema is very similar in taste and texture to sour cream and crème fraîche. It is made by combining buttermilk and heavy cream. Adding the cilantro will give this recipe a nice fresh aftertaste.

Makes 2 cups (475 ml)

In a saucepan, heat the cream over low to medium heat until room temperature. Stir in the buttermilk.

Transfer the mixture to a 1-quart (1-L) mason jar and place the lid on top. Do not seal. Keep the jar on the counter or in a warm place for 24 hours.

Stir in the lime juice and salt, tighten the lid and refrigerate. You will see in a couple of hours how much it has thickened. Add the cilantro and stir, then place back in the refrigerator to thicken.

In a few hours, it will thicken even more. Use immediately or keep covered in the refrigerator for up to 2 weeks.

2 cups (475 ml) heavy cream

2 tbsp (30 ml) buttermilk

Juice of 2 limes

Pinch of salt

1 bunch cilantro, minced

Smoked Salsa Verde

This sauce goes with chicken, pork or even fish dishes. It is a very light and refreshing salsa that gives the best balance to any dish. But my favorite way to use this amazing sauce is on TACOS! Perfect for Taco Tuesday.

Makes 3 to 4 cups (780 g to 1.1 kg)

Soak your wood chips in water for at least 30 minutes. I prefer to let them soak for 2 hours, so you can start this process midday. Make sure you drain the chips well.

Heat your barbecue grill to 400°F (200°C). Remove the husks from the tomatillos.

Cook the tomatillos, onion, jalapeños and serrano peppers on the grill until they are lightly charred on all sides, about 10 minutes. Add your drained wood chips to the grill. Transfer the vegetables back to a baking sheet and drizzle with the olive oil. Place the baking sheet on top of the grill and lower the temperature to 250°F (120°C). Let smoke for 50 minutes.

Remove the vegetables from the grill. Place the peppers in a bowl and cover with plastic wrap. Set aside and let cool. Doing this will make it easier for you to peel the peppers.

Peel the cooled peppers. Remove the stems, cut the peppers in half and remove the membranes.

Remove the seeds from the serrano peppers, but not from the jalapeños; I like to keep them for the heat factor. Cut the tomatillos into large chunks.

In a food processor or blender, combine the tomatillos, garlic, onion and peppers. Add the cilantro and oregano. Pulse to your desired texture; it should be like a chunky salsa. Season with the salt, black pepper and lime juice.

Serve with tortilla chips, burritos, tacos, grilled steaks, chicken, pork or fish.

12 oz (340 g) wood chips, for grill (I like hickory for this recipe)

8 large tomatillos

1 large white onion, cut into quarters

2 jalapeño peppers

2 serrano peppers

2 tbsp (30 ml) olive oil

4 large cloves garlic

1 bunch cilantro

Leaves from 2 sprigs fresh oregano

2 tsp (13 g) kosher salt

1 tsp freshly ground black pepper

¼ cup (60 ml) fresh lime juice

Smoky Salsa

By smoking the tomatoes, you are releasing their oils. I personally prefer a smoky salsa over a regular salsa. The smoke, heat and the natural sweetness from the tomatoes are sure to make this recipe one of your treasures.

Makes 2 cups (520 g)

....

Soak your wood chips in cold water for 30 minutes. Make sure you drain the chips well. Prepare a hot and cold side on your grill—a side with direct heat and one with indirect heat. We want to maintain a temperature of 225°F (110°C).

Place the drained wood chips on the coal. If your grill does not require coal, place the chips in a disposable aluminum foil pan and place near the flames. Place another disposable aluminum foil pan under the unheated side of the grill. Spray the rack on the unheated side with nonstick spray and place the tomatoes, onions, peppers and garlic on that side of the grill. Close the lid and let cook for 1 hour 30 minutes.

Remove the tomatoes, onions, peppers and garlic from the grill. You can either remove the skins of the tomatoes and/or peppers or leave them on. Remove the stems from the peppers and slice the top off the tomato.

In a food processor, combine the tomatoes, onions, peppers and garlic. Pulse until the mixture reaches your desired consistency. Pour the mixture into a bowl and stir in the lime juice, cumin, cilantro, oil and salt. Cover and let cool. Refrigerate until use. Store in the fridge for 3 or 4 days.

12 oz (340 g) wood chips; I like to use apple wood, which gives sweet afternotes

Nonstick spray

5 beefsteak tomatoes

1½ red onions, peeled; cut the whole onion in half

1 jalapeño pepper

1 serrano pepper

2 cloves garlic

Juice of 1 lime

¼ tsp ground cumin

1⅓ cups (55 g) chopped fresh cilantro

1 tsp olive oil

½ tsp salt

Slow and Low Beef Stock

A great stock usually cooks for sixteen-plus hours. Do not be afraid of cooking it too long, because the longer the better. When it's done, you will have a great rewarding feeling come over you. This stock can be frozen in ice cube trays, transferred to ziplock freezer bags, then stored in the freezer for up to 2 months.

Makes 2 to 3 quarts (1.9 to 2.8 L)

Preheat the oven to 450°F (230°C). Spread the veal bones in a roasting pan and roast for about 30 minutes, making sure you flip the bones over at the 15-minute point.

Remove the pan from the oven and brush a thin layer of the tomato paste on the bones, making sure you coat them on all sides. Add your carrots, celery, onions and garlic on top of the bones and return the pan to the oven. Cook for 25 minutes, or until the vegetables are caramelized, making sure you turn the vegetables at around the 12-minute point to get even caramelization.

Transfer the bones and vegetables to a stockpot. Deglaze the roasting pan with the red wine, making sure you scrape the little brown bits on the bottom of the pan. Add this mixture to the stockpot along with the parsley, bay leaves and peppercorns. Cover with 4 quarts (3.8 L) of the cold water.

Let the stock come to a simmer over medium heat. Do not boil. Adjust the heat to a low simmer. Every hour or so, skim off any foam that comes to the top during the first 4 hours. If too much evaporation occurs, add the remaining quart (946 ml) of cold water.

Let the stock cook, uncovered, for a total of 12 hours. For the best results, I like to push it to 18 hours.

Remove the bones and strain the stock through a very fine mesh strainer, or use a colander that has been lined with four layers of cheesecloth. Discard all the solids. Let the stock cool, then refrigerate or freeze in ice cube trays. The stock will keep in the fridge for 1 week, or in the freezer for up to 6 months.

5 lb (2.3 kg) veal bones

8 oz (225 g) tomato paste

4 carrots, peeled and large diced

6 ribs celery, large diced

2 yellow onions, peeled and cut into quarters

4 cloves garlic, smashed

½ cup (120 ml) red wine

1 bunch flat-leaf parsley

3 bay leaves

1 tsp black peppercorns

4 to 5 qt (3.8 to 4.7 L) cold water, divided

Deep-Flavor Chicken Stock

I like to roast my bones to get a darker chicken stock with a much richer flavor. The bay leaves give it a nice balance. Like the beef stock (see headnote, page 134) the chicken stock can be frozen for up to 2 months.

Makes 1½ quarts (1.4 L)

Preheat your oven to 350°F (175°C). Put your chicken carcass on a baking sheet and drizzle with the olive oil. Season with the salt and roast the bones for 30 minutes.

Transfer the bones to a Dutch oven or large stockpot. Add all the remaining ingredients, including the cold water. Bring to a boil for 10 minutes, skim any fat or scum from the top, then lower the heat to low and let cook, covered, for 10 to 12 hours.

Strain the stock and discard all the solids. Let cool down for at least 1 hour. Give a stir and let cool for another hour. Make sure the stock is completely cool before freezing or refrigerating. You can keep in the refrigerator for up to 5 days or in the freezer for 2 months.

1 large chicken carcass (see Notes)

1 tsp olive oil

1 tsp salt

2 yellow onions, peeled and cut into quarters

2 carrots, peeled and cubed

3 ribs celery, cubed

¼ cup (20 g) black peppercorns

4 cloves garlic, smashed

2 qt (1.9 L) cold water

5 bay leaves

Notes: You can reserve any bones from any cooked chicken; this will eliminate the roasting process. If you don't have a carcass, debone 1 large chicken and cut its raw meat into large cubes.

Once the stock has been chilled in the refrigerator you will notice when you take it out that it has a jellylike consistency. This is what you want! Remove the desired amount and reheat to liquefy.

*See photo on page 135.

Go-To Vegetable Broth

You might ask what the difference is between soup stock and broth. Stocks are made with bones. Broths are made with meat. In the case of vegetables, they are always called broth.

This can be kept up to 6 months in your freezer. I suggest freezing this in ice cube trays. Once frozen, transfer to gallon-sized (3.8-L) freezer bags. Take a cube out as needed.

Makes 1½ quarts (1.4 L)

In a stockpot, heat the oil over medium heat and add the celery, carrots, onion, garlic and mushrooms (if using). Sauté the vegetables for 2 minutes.

Add the water and bring to a boil. Add the bay leaves and peppercorns. Once the broth comes to a boil, lower the heat to low and let cook, uncovered, for 5 hours.

Strain the broth, pressing the vegetables with a spoon to extract all the liquid. Discard the vegetables and other solids.

Let cool for 1 hour. Cover and refrigerate for up to 5 days or freeze for up to 2 months.

1 tbsp (15 ml) vegetable oil

3 ribs celery, chopped

2 large carrots, peeled and chopped

1 white onion, unpeeled, chopped

2 cloves garlic, smashed

1 cup (70 g) whole button mushrooms (optional; see Note)

2 qt (1.9 L) water

2 bay leaves

1 tsp black peppercorns

Note: The mushrooms give the broth another level of earthiness.

*See photo on page 135.

The Best BBQ Sauce

I have spent years and years trying to make the best barbecue sauce out there. In my opinion, this recipe has everything you need. It is well balanced between sweet, spicy and tangy. It goes great with anything—fish, ribs, pork, chicken or beef. Store leftovers in an airtight container for up to 3 weeks.

Makes 2 to 4 cups (475 to 946 ml)

In a large pot, whisk together all the ingredients. Bring to a boil, then lower the heat to low. Let cook, uncovered, for 4 hours. Remove from the heat, let cool and store in an airtight container.

1 cup (225 g) light brown sugar

1 cup (240 ml) apple cider

½ cup (75 g) minced garlic

½ cup (80 g) minced onion

1 (8-oz [226-g]) can tomato sauce

½ cup (120 ml) Worcestershire sauce

3 cups (710 ml) ketchup

2 tbsp (12 g) freshly ground black pepper

2 tbsp (30 g) molasses

1 tsp liquid smoke

2 tbsp (36 g) salt

1 tsp cayenne pepper

1 cup (240 ml) cola

1 tbsp (9 g) garlic powder

1 tsp dry mustard

1 tsp smoked paprika

1 tsp onion powder

2 cups (475 ml) water

Desserts,
Please!

· ·

Who doesn't love dessert? The desserts that I picked for this book are by far my absolute favorites to make. Some of the recipes might be long, but they are not as hard as they look. They will soon become treasures in your recipe bible and I promise you they are well worth the wait.

Chocolate Pot de Crème

This by far my favorite dessert to make because it's super easy to prepare. I make this at almost every event I do. It's simple and foolproof, and the flavors are rich and velvety.

Serves 6

Melt the semisweet and dark chocolate in a double boiler. If you don't have a double boiler, fill a pot halfway with water and heat it over high heat until the water comes to a simmer. Lower the heat to low, then place a large, heatproof bowl atop the pot (make sure it is not touching the water), and let the chocolate melt in the bowl.

In a separate saucepan, combine the milk and cream and bring to a slight simmer.

In a large bowl, whisk together the egg yolks, sugar, salt and vanilla bean seeds and extract. *Slowly* pour the cream mixture, 2 tablespoons (30 ml) at a time, into the egg mixture to temper it, making sure you are whisking the egg mixture at the same time, to avoid cooking the eggs to scrambled.

Pour the mixture into the saucepan that had been used to heat the cream mixture and cook over low heat for 5 minutes. The mixture should be able to coat the back of a spoon. Pour in the melted chocolate and whisk until smooth.

Pour into individual cups or a 12-ounce (355-ml) casserole dish. Preheat the oven to 200°F (90°C). If portioned into individual cups, place in a casserole dish large enough to hold the cups and fill the casserole with water until it comes halfway up the outside of each cup. If using a casserole dish, place in a larger casserole dish and fill the outer dish halfway up with water. Bake for 4 hours.

Remove from the oven and let cool for 15 minutes before removing the cups or casserole from the water bath and letting cool on a wire rack. Place in the refrigerator and chill for 5 hours.

My favorite way to serve this is to place marshmallows on top of the chocolate pudding and toast them under the broiler. It's like adult s'mores!

18 oz (510 g) semisweet chocolate, chopped

8 oz (225 g) dark chocolate, chopped

2 cups (475 ml) whole milk

3 cups (710 ml) heavy cream

12 large egg yolks

1½ cups (300 g) sugar

1 tsp fine salt

1 fresh vanilla bean, sliced in half and scraped

2 tsp (10 ml) vanilla extract

Rocky Road Cake

Chocolate is one of my favorite things to eat besides cake and donuts. I learned this particular version of how to make a chocolate cake from an old pastry chef friend of mine when I was just a line cook. I like to use three different types of chocolate for the frosting, which gives it that rich flavor. I put marshmallows and nuts in between the two layers so you can enjoy the rockiness in each bite.

Serves 6 to 8

....

Prepare the cake: Preheat your oven to 250°F (120°C). Place the racks in the center of the oven to ensure even cooking. Spray two 8-inch (20-cm) round pans with nonstick spray and set aside.

In a bowl, sift together the flour, baking powder, baking soda, salt and cocoa powder and set aside.

In the bowl of an electric mixer, combine the granulated sugar and eggs. Beat together on medium speed until the mixture is a pale yellow, also known as the ribbon stage, about 5 minutes. Add the mayonnaise, espresso and vanilla and beat until smooth, making sure to scrape down the sides. Add one-third of the dry mixture and mix on low speed to incorporate, add another third of the dry mixture and mix well, then add the final third of the dry mixture and mix. Scrape, scrape, scrape. Don't forget to scrape the sides down.

Divide the batter evenly between the prepared cake pans. Place in the center of the oven and bake for 4 hours, or until the cake springs back from your touch or has an internal temperature of 200°F (90°C). Remove the pans from the oven and let the cake cool in its pans on a wire rack while you prepare the frosting and ganache.

Prepare the frosting: Let the sour cream sit out at room temperature to get the chill off. Use a double boiler to melt all the chocolate chips for the frosting along with the butter. When the mixture is fully melted and smooth, add the sour cream. Whisk together until the frosting is smooth. Add the salt and vanilla at this time. Sift in the confectioners' sugar and whisk until shiny and smooth. Set aside.

(Continued)

Chocolate Cake

Nonstick spray

2 cups (250 g) all-purpose flour

1 tsp baking powder

½ tsp baking soda

1 tsp kosher salt

¾ cup (83 g) unsweetened cocoa powder

2 cups (400 g) granulated sugar

2 large eggs

1 cup (225 g) mayonnaise

1 tbsp (15 ml) brewed espresso

2 tsp (10 ml) pure vanilla extract

Yummy Frosting

1 cup (230 g) sour cream

¾ cup (131 g) semisweet chocolate chips

¾ cup (131 g) dark chocolate chips

¾ cup (131 g) milk chocolate chips

½ cup (112 g/1 stick) unsalted butter

¼ tsp salt

1 tsp vanilla extract

2 cups (240 g) confectioners' sugar

Prepare the ganache: In a small saucepan, heat the chocolate chips, cream, vanilla and salt over low to medium heat until all the chocolate is completely melted and the mixture is smooth. Set aside.

To assemble: When the cakes are completely cool, place one round on a plate. With an offset spatula, evenly spread one-third of the frosting on the top of the round. Then add 1 cup (50 g) of marshmallows and 1 cup (100 g) of nuts on top. Place the second cake round on top of the first to form two layers. Then, use the offset spatula to spread the rest of the frosting on top of the cake and around the sides, making sure the frosting is evenly distributed. When you are finished icing the cake, now comes the fun part: Pour the liquid ganache onto the middle of the cake and spread it out with the offset spatula. It is okay if some falls off the edges; that is what you want. Like raindrops of ganache.

Time to throw the remaining marshmallows and nuts wherever you like on the cake. Make it abstract.

Chocolate Ganache

½ cup (88 g) semisweet chocolate chips

½ cup (120 ml) heavy cream

½ tsp vanilla extract

Pinch of salt

2 cups (100 g) mini marshmallows, divided

2 cups (200 g) nuts, toasted and coarsely chopped, divided

Gooey Monkey Bread

Who says you have to be a kid to enjoy this. This might look a bit complicated, but I promise you that it is worth it. You can cheat by using biscuit dough from your grocery store, but I find it more satisfying to make my own dough. There is no monkeying around this. It might be smart to make two. You will see why . . .

Serves 6 to 8

Prepare the dough: Preheat your oven to 175°F (80°C). Spray an ovenproof glass bowl with nonstick spray and set aside. In another glass bowl, combine the warm water, instant yeast, 1 tablespoon (13 g) of the granulated sugar and the melted butter and salt. Mix and set aside for at least 5 minutes. When the yeast is fully dissolved and starts to foam, you know your yeast is ready.

In the stand mixer bowl, combine the flour and remaining granulated sugar. Turn the mixer on low speed. Add the yeast mixture slowly, followed by the warm milk. Increase the speed to medium and mix until none of the dough is sticking to the sides of the bowl. If it still seems a bit wet, add more flour, 1 tablespoon (7 g) at a time. Mix for at least 6 minutes.

When finished mixing, transfer the dough to the sprayed glass bowl. Shut off the oven and put the glass bowl, covered with a clean towel, in the oven to rise for 1 hour. The dough should rise twice its size.

While the dough is rising, begin to prepare the coating: In one bowl, combine the cinnamon, brown sugar and granulated sugar. In a second bowl, combine the melted butter with the vanilla. Set both bowls aside.

When the dough is finished rising, place on a lightly floured work space and push it down. Roll out until you have a 9-inch (23-cm) square. Spray a Bundt pan with nonstick spray, making sure you get every little spot. Cut the dough into 1-inch (2.5-cm) pieces. Roll each piece into a ball (they don't need to be perfectly round but close enough). Dip each ball in the melted butter mixture and then roll in the cinnamon mixture. Layer the balls in the Bundt pan. Continue doing this until all balls are evenly distributed throughout the pan.

(Continued)

Dough

Nonstick spray

¼ cup (60 ml) water, warm (105 to 115°F [41 to 46°C])

1 (0.25-oz [8-g]) packet instant yeast

⅓ cup (67 g) granulated sugar, divided

2 tbsp (28 g) unsalted butter, melted

1 tsp salt

3½ cups (438 g) all-purpose flour, plus more if needed and for dusting

1¼ cups (295 ml) whole milk, warm (105 to 115°F [41 to 46°C])

Coating

1 tbsp (7 g) ground cinnamon

1 cup (225 g) light brown sugar

¾ cup (150 g) granulated sugar

1 cup (225 g) unsalted butter, melted

1 tsp vanilla extract

Gooey Monkey Bread
continued

Cover the Bundt pan with plastic wrap and put in a warm place for the dough to rise. It usually takes an hour for the dough to reach the top of the Bundt pan.

While the dough is rising, preheat your oven to 200°F (90°C). I like to cook my bread at a low temperature to achieve the fluffiest monkey bread. Place the pan in the oven and cook the bread for 6 hours at 200°F (90°C). Increase the heat to 350°F (175°C) and continue to cook until the top browns, usually 15 minutes. You should see the bubbling of the butter and sugar on top.

Remove from the oven and let cool in the pan. If you choose to make the glaze, you would do so now: In a small bowl, combine the milk and confectioners' sugar. When the monkey bread has cooled for 10 minutes, place a large plate on top of the Bundt pan. Flip over so the monkey bread is standing upright. Remove the pan and pour the glaze over the bread, if desired.

Glaze (optional)

3 tbsp (45 ml) milk

¾ cup (90 g) confectioners' sugar

Deep-Fried Bread Pudding

If you caught my *Chopped* episode, "Tendon Intentions," you would have seen me throw this together in 30 minutes. But I prefer to cook it the slow and low way. Making bread pudding at my restaurant, I am able to keep food costs down by using all the old bread to make this decadent bread pudding. For this recipe I use challah, but you really can make it with any type of white bread.

Serves 6 to 8

In a bowl, soak the cranberries in the orange juice. I like to have them soak for at least 1 hour. In a separate bowl, mix together the granulated sugar, milk, eggs, baking powder, salt, cinnamon and the vanilla bean and extract. Throw in your bread pieces and toss with the milk mixture.

Drain the cranberries and toss into the bread mixture along with the white chocolate chips. Cover and refrigerate for 24 hours. Trust me; you will thank me.

Preheat your oven to 225°F (110°C). Take your bread pudding from the refrigerator and let it come to room temperature. Spray the inner surfaces of a Dutch oven with nonstick spray to evenly coat the pot. Transfer the bread mixture to the prepared pot and make sure it is evenly spread out.

Cover and place on the center rack in the oven. Cook for 2 hours 30 minutes. Remove from the oven and let cool. Remove the pudding from the Dutch oven and continue to let cool on a baking rack.

Heat the oil in a deep fryer to 350°F (175°C). If you don't have a portable tabletop fryer, you can use a 4-quart (3.8-L) pot: Pour in the oil and place over medium heat. Let the oil heat up for 10 minutes.

Time to make the glaze . . . ready . . . mix the cold milk with the confectioners' sugar. Boom, you're done!

Cut the bread pudding into 1-inch (2.5-cm) cubes. Now it's time for the magic. Add several pieces at a time to the fryer. Try not to overcrowd the fryer. Let cook for 3 minutes. Remove from the oil and drain on a paper towel. Top with the confectioners' sugar and the glaze. This goes great with any ice cream!

Bread Pudding

½ cup (60 g) dried cranberries

1 cup (240 ml) orange juice

1½ cups (300 g) granulated sugar

1 qt (1 L) milk

6 large eggs, beaten

2 tsp (9 g) baking powder

1 tsp salt

2 tsp (5 g) ground cinnamon

1 whole vanilla bean, cut in half and scraped

1 tsp vanilla extract

1 loaf challah (day old or 2 days old is best), cut into 1" (2.5-cm) cubes

½ cup (88 g) white chocolate chips

Nonstick spray

2 qt (1.9 L) vegetable oil, for frying

½ cup (60 g) confectioners' sugar

Glaze

¼ cup (60 ml) cold milk

1 cup (120 g) confectioners' sugar

Slow-Cooked Blueberry Cobbler

Something about slow cooking this ooey-gooey blueberry deliciousness really brings out the freshness of any blueberry, be it frozen or fresh. It comes out amazing every time.

Serves 6

Preheat your oven to 225°F (110°C).

Prepare the blueberries: Heat a Dutch oven over low heat. Add the butter and melt. Stir in the blueberries, vanilla, sugar, salt, water and ground ginger. Let cook for 5 minutes, or until the mixture reaches a syruplike consistency. Add the lemon zest, juice and flour. Bring to a quick boil, then turn off the heat. Remove the pot from the heat. Throw in the fresh basil.

Prepare the crust: In a bowl, stir together the flour, cinnamon and baking powder. Add your melted butter, whole milk, buttermilk and egg and stir to form a batter.

Pour your batter evenly on top of the blueberries. This will make a crust.

Put the Dutch oven in the center of the oven and cook for 5 hours 30 minutes. Increase the oven temperature to 350°F (175°C) and cook the cobbler for another 10 minutes to get golden brown on top.

Blueberries

2 tbsp (28 g) unsalted butter

2 cups (290 g) fresh blueberries

1 tsp vanilla extract

½ cup (100 g) sugar

¼ tsp salt

¼ cup (60 ml) water

½ tsp ground ginger

2 tsp (6 g) lemon zest

1 tsp fresh lemon juice

¼ cup (30 g) all-purpose flour

1 tsp fresh basil

Crust

1 cup (125 g) all-purpose flour

1 tsp ground cinnamon

1 tsp baking powder

2 tbsp (28 g) unsalted butter, melted

½ cup (120 ml) whole milk

¼ cup (60 ml) buttermilk

1 large egg, beaten

Acknowledgments

First, I want to start off and say thank you to my mom and dad. Mom, you are my best friend and have always been there for me no matter what. Thank you for always being in my corner and guiding me through life. I thank you for making me the woman I am today.

Dad, I want to say thank you for helping me with my business and for making me the competitive person I am today. The weekends playing basketball or softball always pushed me to be better and stronger.

Vita, you are the best sister anyone could ever have. I am grateful every day that I have a best friend and a sister like you in my corner. You are the calm one out of all of us and because of this I will always take your advice. Thank you for having my back!

To my publishing company, thank you for believing in me and taking my book on.

Marissa Giambelluca, my editor, thank you for having patience with me while I wrote this book. I appreciate all the guidance you have given me. To Meg Palmer, Meg Baskis and the rest of Page Street, thank you!

Jennifer Blume, thank you for being the best photographer and putting me in contact with Page Street.

Lisa Betters, thank you for putting me in contact with José A. Villar-Portela to help me edit my book.

Chef Dewey Losasso, for being the best mentor a kid could have.

Lori Flynn, who was one of my culinary instructors who was hard and fair. She knew before I did that my path was going to be adventurous.

Thank you to my best friends Lauren Parisi and Krysta Harrison for always being there for me and pushing me to the limits.

About the Author

With a half Puerto Rican, half Italian background, Robyn Almodovar's childhood was filled with culture, vibrancy and a deeply ingrained passion for food that began in Staten Island.

In 2005, Almodovar graduated from Le Cordon Bleu College of Culinary Arts in Atlanta and relocated to Fort Lauderdale, Florida, to begin her apprenticeship as a banquet cook at the Hyatt Regency Pier 66, a Four Diamond Hotel.

In 2008, Almodovar took to the high seas and became the executive chef of a 172-foot (52-m) yacht, *Lady Windridge*. She spent her days as a yacht chef for two and a half years then she worked at several respectable South Florida restaurants, including the Forge and Danny Devito's Devito South Beach before obtaining an executive sous chef position at the Royal Palm Hotel. That is when she was cast for FOX's *Hell's Kitchen* Season 10 and finished as a top finalist.

In 2011, Almodovar purchased a 24-foot (7-m) food truck and founded Palate Party, a fresh, mobile food café that utilizes locally sourced ingredients. Palate Party was the first female-owned, non-dessert food truck in South Florida, and in 2013, *Miami New Times* voted Palate Party Best Food Truck in Miami; it was also voted Third Best Food Truck in South Florida by the *Sun Sentinel*.

In the fall of 2014, Almodovar was on a new television series, *Food Truck Face Off*, on Food Network. Almodovar was the Miami Food Truck Expert guest judge for three episodes. In July and August of 2015, Chef Robyn Almodovar competed in and won both *Chopped* and *Cutthroat Kitchen*, both on Food Network. Almodovar was also a contestant in July 2015 on *Camp Cutthroat*. In September 2015, Almodovar was a contestant on *Chopped Impossible*.

In 2016, Almodovar joined forces with Sea Delight and became its chef ambassador, educating sales reps and cooks at conventions in Brussels, Amsterdam, Boston, New York and Los Angeles.

In 2017, Chef Gordon Ramsay called and personally invited Robyn to be a contestant on *Hell's Kitchen All Stars* Season 17. Almodovar accepted the offer and although she did not win, she placed fifth and regained the prestigious black jacket. Almodovar continues to strive as a culinarian, a brand ambassador and a rising restaurateur. She feels that as long as there are local purveyors, she can give anyone bold and vibrant flavors.

Index

A

All about That Bisque, 84
andouille sausage, 83
Apple & Celeriac Salad, 68
apple juice, 47
arugula, 46, 95, 100
Asian Slaw, 60

B

bacon. *See also* pancetta
    Beefed Up Bourguignon, 75
    Chicken Chasseur, 42
    Lamb & Squash Soup, 79
    Southern Collard Greens, 116
    Sweet and Spicy Baked Beans, 115
baked beans, 115
BBQ sauce, 139
beans
    Cassoulet, My Way, 33–34
    Cuban Black Beans, 112
    Healthy, Hearty Spinach, Sausage &
        Bean Soup, 83
    Lamb & Squash Soup, 79
    Puerto Rican Red Beans, 108
    Short Rib Chili, 93–94
    Sweet and Spicy Baked Beans, 115
beef stock, 134
Beefed Up Bourguignon, 75
beer, 26, 93–94
bell peppers
    Asian Slaw, 60
    Grandma's Beef Stew, 21
    Lamb & Squash Soup, 79
    Momma Duke's Chicken Tacos, 22

Puerto Rican Red Beans, 108
Ropa Vieja, 25
Short Rib Chili, 93–94
Best BBQ Sauce, The, 139
Best Indoor Brisket, The, 38
Best Meat Sliders Around, The, 90
bisque, 84
black beans, 112
blue cheese, 32
blueberry cobbler, 153
bok choy, 60
bones, 12–14, 116, 134
Bourguignon, 75
bread, 107
bread pudding, 150
brisket, 38
broccoli, 32, 60
Broccoli and Brussels Slaw, 32
broth, 137
Brussels sprouts, 32
Burrata, 46

C

cabbage, 60, 71
cake, 144–146
cannellini beans, 33–34
carrots, 11, 60, 134
Cassoulet, My Way, 33–34
celeriac, 68–69
celery, 11, 66, 68–69
challah bread, 147–149
chasseur, 42
cheddar cheese, 65, 76
cheese. *See individual types*

chicken
    Cassoulet, My Way, 33–34
    Chicken Chasseur, 42
    Game Day Wings, 89
    Momma Duke's Chicken Tacos, 22
    Puerto Rican Chicken Stew, 15–17
    Rich and Velvety Coq au Vin, 37
    Sticky Drumsticks, 95
    Take That Chicken and Throw It on
        Top of a Beer, 26
Chicken Chasseur, 42
chicken stock, 136
chiles, 52, 93–94
chili, 93–94
chimichurri, 52
chipotle peppers in adobo sauce, 22,
        93–94
chocolate, 143, 144–146, 150
Chocolate Pot de Crème, 143
chowder, 80
Cilantro-Lime Crema, 129
Citrus-Smoked Salmon, 41
Classic Crema, 126
cobbler, 153
cod, 52
cola, 76, 99, 139
collard greens, 116
coq au vin, 37
corn, 80, 119
corn chowder, 80
cornbread, 111
Cotija cheese, 71
cranberries, 147–149
crema, 126, 129
Cuban Black Beans, 112
custard, 143

D

Deep-Flavor Chicken Stock, 136
Deep-Fried Bread Pudding, 150
desserts
    Chocolate Pot de Crème, 143
    Deep-Fried Bread Pudding, 150
    Gooey Monkey Bread, 147–149
    Rocky Road Cake, 144–146
    Slow-Cooked Blueberry Cobbler,
       153
dinners
    Best Indoor Brisket, The, 38
    Cassoulet, My Way, 33–34
    Chicken Chasseur, 42
    Citrus-Smoked Salmon, 41
    Duck Confit with Apple & Celeriac
      Salad, 68–69
    Lamb Shank with Orange
      Gremolata, 66
    Momma Duke's Chicken Tacos, 22
    Not Yo Momma's Meatloaf, 18
    Not Your Ordinary Pot Roast, 11
    Nothing Baby about These Ribs with
      Burrata and Peach Salad,
      45–46
    Pork Belly Tacos, 71
    Pork Belly This, 51
    Rich and Velvety Coq au Vin, 37
    Ropa Vieja, 25
    Sausage & Gravy Pizza, 61–62
    Set-and-Forget It Quiche, 65
    Slow-Roasted Cod with
      Chimichurri, 52
    Slow-Roasted Pork Butt with Sweet
      & Spicy Glaze, 55
    Slow-Smoked Beef Ribs, 56
    Smoked Ham Shank with
      Watermelon Relish, 47–48
    Soy-Marinated Short Ribs with
      Asian Slaw, 59–60
    Standout Pork Shank with Broccoli
      and Brussels Sprout Slaw,
      31–32
    Sunday Gravy and Meatballs, 12–14
    Take That Chicken and Throw It on
      Top of a Beer, 26
Dr Pepper, 55
dressings, 46
drumsticks, 95
Duck Confit with Apple & Celeriac
    Salad, 68–69
Dutch Oven Bread, 107

E

eggs, 61–62, 65, 103
empanadas, 103
espresso, 144–146

F

frosting, 144–146

G

Game Day Wings, 89
ganache, 144–146
glazes, 55, 149, 150
goat cheese, 65, 95
Gooey Monkey Bread, 147–149
Go-To Vegetable Broth, 137
Grandma's Beef Stew, 21
gravy, 12–14
great northern beans, 83
ground beef, 12–14, 18, 90
Gruyère cheese, 76
Guinness, 93–94

H

ham, 33–34, 47, 116
Healthy, Hearty Spinach, Sausage &
    Bean Soup, 83
honey, 95
hot sauce, 125

J

Jack cheese, 103
jalapeño peppers
    Asian Slaw, 60
    Short Rib Chili, 93–94
    Smoked Salsa Verde, 130
    Smoky Salsa, 133
    Watermelon Relish, 48
juniper berries, 68–69

K

kale, 79
Kickin' Cornbread, 111

L

Lamb Shank with Orange Gremolata, 66
Lamb & Squash Soup, 79
lemons
    Broccoli and Brussels Slaw, 32
    Citrus-Smoked Salmon, 41
    Duck Confit with Apple & Celeriac
      Salad, 68–69
    Slow-Roasted Cod with
      Chimichurri, 52
    Slow-Roasted Pork Sandwich, 100
limes
    Citrus-Smoked Salmon, 41
    Short Rib Chili, 93–94
    Smoked Salsa Verde, 130
    Smoky Salsa, 133
    Soy-Marinated Short Ribs, 59
lobsters, 84

M

mac and cheese, 76
maple syrup, 47, 55
marshmallows, 144–146
meatballs, 14, 90
meatloaf, 18
mint, 48
Momma Duke's Chicken Tacos, 22
monkey bread, 147–149
mozzarella cheese, 90
mushrooms
    Beefed Up Bourguignon, 75
    Chicken Chasseur, 42
    Cuban Black Beans, 112
    Go-To Vegetable Broth, 137
    My Momma's Mushrooms, 120
    Rich and Velvety Coq au Vin, 37
My Famous Wing Sauce, 125
My Momma's Mushrooms, 120

N

northern beans, 83
Not Yo Momma's Meatloaf, 18
Not Your Ordinary Pot Roast, 11
Nothing Baby about These Ribs with
    Burrata and Peach Salad,
    45–46
nuts, 32, 144–146

O

olives
    Grandma's Beef Stew, 21
    Puerto Rican Chicken Stew, 15–17
    Puerto Rican Red Beans, 108
    Ropa Vieja, 25
    Ropa Vieja Empanadas, 103

onions
    Beefed Up Bourguignon, 75
    Deep-Flavor Chicken Stock, 136
    Not Your Ordinary Pot Roast, 11
    Piggy Mac, 76
    Slow and Low Beef Stock, 134
    Slow-Roasted Pork Sandwich, 100
    Smoked Salsa Verde, 130
    Smoky Salsa, 133
    Southern Collard Greens, 116
Orange Gremolata, 66
orange juice, 147–149
oranges, 41, 66, 68–69

P

pancetta, 37. See also bacon
Parmesan cheese
    Best Meat Sliders Around, The, 90
    Broccoli and Brussels Slaw, 32
    Set-and-Forget It Quiche, 65
    Sunday Gravy, 12–14
parsley, 66
party food
    Best Meat Sliders Around, The, 90
    Game Day Wings, 89
    Ropa Vieja Empanadas, 103
    Short Rib Chili with Cornbread,
        93–94
    Slow-Roasted Pork Sandwich, 100
    Sticky Drumsticks with Watermelon
        Salad, 95–96
    2-Stepin' Spare Ribs, 99
pasta, 76
peaches, 46
peppers. See individual types
Piggy Mac, 76
pineapple, 71
pinto beans, 79, 115

pizza, 61–62
pork. See also bacon; ham; pancetta;
        sausage
    Cassoulet, My Way, 33–34
    Piggy Mac, 76
    Pork Belly Tacos, 71
    Pork Belly This, 51
    Slow-Roasted Pork Butt with Sweet
        & Spicy Glaze, 55
    Standout Pork Shank, 31–32
Pork Belly Tacos, 71
Pork Belly This, 51
pot roast, 11
potatoes
    Beefed Up Bourguignon, 75
    Grandma's Beef Stew, 21
    Not Your Ordinary Pot Roast, 11
    Puerto Rican Chicken Stew, 15–17
    Puerto Rican Red Beans, 108
    Ropa Vieja, 25
    Smoked Corn Chowder, 80
provolone cheese, 76, 90
Puerto Rican Chicken Stew, 15–17
Puerto Rican Red Beans, 108

R

red beans, 93–94, 108
relishes, 48, 119
ribs
    2-Steppin' Spare Ribs, 99
    Nothing Baby about These Ribs, 45
    Short Rib Chili, 93–94
    Slow-Smoked Beef Ribs, 56
    Soy-Marinated Short Ribs, 59
Rich and Velvety Coq au Vin, 37
roast, 11
Rocky Road Cake, 144–146
Ropa Vieja, 25
Ropa Vieja Empanadas, 103

S

salads, 46, 68, 96
salmon, 41
salsas, 130, 133
sandwiches, 90, 100
sauces, 125, 139. *See also* glazes
sausage
    Cassoulet, My Way, 33–34
    Healthy, Hearty Spinach, Sausage &
        Bean Soup, 83
    Sausage & Gravy Pizza, 61–62
    Set-and-Forget It Quiche, 65
    Sunday Gravy, 12–14
    Sweet and Spicy Baked Beans, 115
Sausage & Gravy Pizza, 61–62
seafood, 41, 52, 84
serrano peppers, 115, 130, 133
Set-and-Forget It Quiche, 65
Short Rib Chili with Cornbread, 93–94
side dishes
    Asian Slaw, 60
    Broccoli and Brussels Slaw, 32
    Cuban Black Beans, 112
    Dutch Oven Bread, 107
    Kickin' Cornbread, 111
    My Momma's Mushrooms, 120
    Puerto Rican Red Beans, 108
    Southern Collard Greens, 116
    Sweet and Spicy Baked Beans, 115
sliders, 90
Slow and Low Beef Stock, 134
Slow-Cooked Blueberry Cobbler, 153
Slow-Roasted Cod with Chimichurri, 52
Slow-Roasted Pork Butt with Sweet &
    Spicy Glaze, 55
Slow-Roasted Pork Sandwich, 100
Slow-Smoked Beef Ribs, 56
Smoked Corn Chowder, 80
Smoked & Grilled Corn Relish, 119
Smoked Ham Shank with Watermelon
    Relish, 47–48

Smoked Salsa Verde, 130
Smoky Salsa, 133
soups and stews
    All about That Bisque, 84
    Beefed Up Bourguignon, 75
    Grandma's Beef Stew, 21
    Healthy, Hearty Spinach, Sausage &
        Bean Soup, 83
    Lamb & Squash Soup, 79
    Puerto Rican Chicken Stew, 15–17
    Smoked Corn Chowder, 80
Southern Collard Greens, 116
Soy-Marinated Short Ribs with Asian
    Slaw, 59–60
Spicy Baked Beans, 26
spinach, 65, 83
squash, 79
Standout Pork Shank with Broccoli and
    Brussels Sprout Slaw, 31–32
stews. *See* soups and stews
Sticky Drumsticks with Watermelon
    Salad, 95–96
stocks and broths, 134, 136, 137
Sunday Gravy, 12–14
sunflower seeds, 95
Sweet and Spicy Baked Beans, 115

T

tacos, 22, 71
Take That Chicken and Throw It on Top
    of a Beer, 26
tomatillos, 130
tomatoes
    Chicken Chasseur, 42
    Short Rib Chili, 93–94
    Slow-Roasted Cod with
        Chimichurri, 52
    Smoky Salsa, 133
    2-Steppin' Spare Ribs, 99

V

veal bones, 134
vegetable broth, 137

W

walnuts, 32
Watermelon Relish, 48
Watermelon Salad, 96
wine
    red, 37, 66, 75, 134
    white, 31–32, 33–34
wings, 89